M000239340

SUCCEEDING WITH AGILE HYBRIDS

PROJECT DELIVERY USING HYBRID METHODOLOGIES

Shawn Belling

Thanks for reading.

Shawn D. Bell

Apress®

Succeeding with Agile Hybrids

Shawn Belling
Fitchburg, WI, USA

ISBN-13 (pbk): 978-1-4842-6460-7   ISBN-13 (electronic): 978-1-4842-6461-4
https://doi.org/10.1007/978-1-4842-6461-4

Copyright © 2020 by Shawn Belling

This work is subject to copyright. All rights are reserved by the Publisher, whether the whole or part of the material is concerned, specifically the rights of translation, reprinting, reuse of illustrations, recitation, broadcasting, reproduction on microfilms or in any other physical way, and transmission or information storage and retrieval, electronic adaptation, computer software, or by similar or dissimilar methodology now known or hereafter developed.

Trademarked names, logos, and images may appear in this book. Rather than use a trademark symbol with every occurrence of a trademarked name, logo, or image we use the names, logos, and images only in an editorial fashion and to the benefit of the trademark owner, with no intention of infringement of the trademark.

The use in this publication of trade names, trademarks, service marks, and similar terms, even if they are not identified as such, is not to be taken as an expression of opinion as to whether or not they are subject to proprietary rights.

While the advice and information in this book are believed to be true and accurate at the date of publication, neither the authors nor the editors nor the publisher can accept any legal responsibility for any errors or omissions that may be made. The publisher makes no warranty, express or implied, with respect to the material contained herein.

Managing Director, Apress Media LLC: Welmoed Spahr
Acquisitions Editor: Shiva Ramachandran
Development Editor: James Markham
Coordinating Editor: Nancy Chen

Cover designed by eStudioCalamar

Distributed to the book trade worldwide by Springer Science+Business Media New York, 1 New York Plaza, New York, NY 100043. Phone 1-800-SPRINGER, fax (201) 348-4505, e-mail orders-ny@springer-sbm.com, or visit www.springeronline.com. Apress Media, LLC is a California LLC and the sole member (owner) is Springer Science + Business Media Finance Inc (SSBM Finance Inc). SSBM Finance Inc is a **Delaware** corporation.

For information on translations, please e-mail booktranslations@springernature.com; for reprint, paperback, or audio rights, please e-mail bookpermissions@springernature.com.

Apress titles may be purchased in bulk for academic, corporate, or promotional use. eBook versions and licenses are also available for most titles. For more information, reference our Print and eBook Bulk Sales web page at http://www.apress.com/bulk-sales.

Any source code or other supplementary material referenced by the author in this book is available to readers on GitHub via the book's product page, located at www.apress.com/978-1-4842-6460-7. For more detailed information, please visit http://www.apress.com/source-code.

Printed on acid-free paper

This book is dedicated to my wife, Jody, with thanks and recognition for her warm encouragement and constant support of this and all of my endeavors.

A dedication also goes to the late Dr. Ginger Levin. Ginger was a teacher and mentor to me as well as an inspiration. Ginger set the bar high as a professor and an author. Thanks, Ginger.

Contents

About the Author

Shawn Belling is a globally experienced technology executive and project management speaker and instructor. In a career spanning 30 years, he has held executive and leadership roles in higher education, software, consulting, biopharma, manufacturing, and regulatory compliance and is currently the chief information officer at a large regional technical college.

As a member of the Project Management Institute, he has spoken regularly at conferences and seminars since 2008, which include multiple presentations at PMI Global Conferences in the United States and APAC.

Shawn teaches at the University of Wisconsin–Madison in Engineering Professional Development and the Center for Executive and Professional Development, at the University of Wisconsin–Platteville in the Master of Science Project Management program, and at the University of Southern California in the Master of Science Project Management program.

Shawn is certified by PMI as a Project Management Professional and Agile Certified Practitioner, is a Certified Scrum Professional and Certified Scrum@ Scale Practitioner, and is certified in Organizational Change Leadership from the University of Wisconsin–Platteville.

Shawn earned undergraduate and graduate degrees from the University of Wisconsin schools and is completing a doctorate in leadership.

Acknowledgments

Thanks to David Antonioni, PhD, former program director at the University of Wisconsin's Executive Education program in Project Management who gave me an opportunity to teach back in 2001. I am forever indebted to David for this first opportunity to teach at the University of Wisconsin.

Thanks goes to Scott Converse, program director of the Wisconsin School of Business Center for Professional and Executive Development's project management program, for his collaboration and support of course development and delivery of agile and scrum methodologies since 2011.

Thanks to D.W. (Bill) Haskins, program director for the Master of Science in Project Management program at the University of Wisconsin–Platteville, for affording me the opportunity to teach in the master of science in project management program since 2008 and develop and teach the agile project management course since 2012.

Finally, I wish to acknowledge and thank the many trainers, coworkers, and students with whom I have had the privilege of learning from, working with, and teaching throughout my career. Learning is a lifelong process, and one through which we are always giving and receiving no matter what role one is in.

Introduction

This book is a synthesis of my practical experience, education, and training as a practitioner and instructor in hybrid agile frameworks and practices. This book sources material from courses I have developed and taught, presentations I have developed, and articles I have written for various publications.

The intent of this book is to provide insights and ideas on the practical application of agile frameworks, practices, and techniques to successfully deliver projects using hybrid approaches – which is what the majority of organizations attempting to implement agile end up practicing. It is not intended to provide a purist approach to any particular agile framework. This book sources and credits agile frameworks and their authors or notable trainers frequently while focusing on practical hybrid applications.

This book will discuss hybrid agile from a practical perspective, with examples from real-life scenarios and from the perspectives of key agile roles and behaviors. The book will provide the practitioner with patterns and examples to use in modeling their own understanding and implementation of agile practices and hopefully help make the journey a bit easier.

This book assumes that the reader has some familiarity and initial experience with agile project management practices as well as waterfall project management. A reader of this book may derive more benefit by being less versed in a particular flavor of agile and more open to the practical benefits of being methodology-agnostic and simply using and applying what could work in their own organizations and applications.

Agile Hybrids

Defining Agile Hybrids

The continuum — where we *really* work

My experience is that most organizations find themselves somewhere on a continuum between plan-driven (a.k.a. waterfall) project management and agile project management. An organization's place on the continuum is driven by a variety of factors. Many organizations find themselves using a hybrid approach somewhere on that continuum — one that considers these factors and offers benefits from both waterfall and agile (Figure 1-1).

© Shawn Belling 2020
S. Belling, *Succeeding with Agile Hybrids*, https://doi.org/10.1007/978-1-4842-6461-4_1

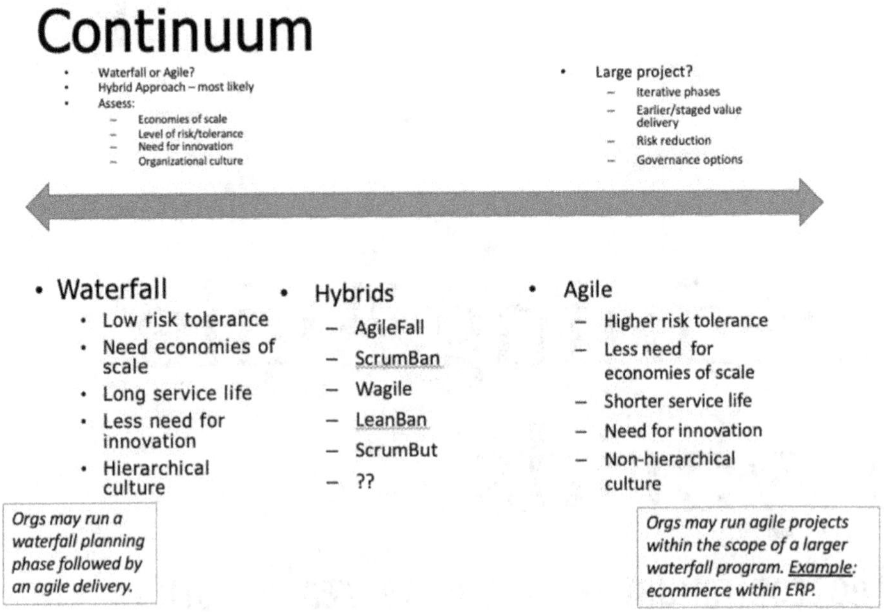

Continuum

- Waterfall or Agile?
- Hybrid Approach – most likely
- Assess:
  - Economies of scale
  - Level of risk/tolerance
  - Need for innovation
  - Organizational culture

- Large project?
  - Iterative phases
  - Earlier/staged value delivery
  - Risk reduction
  - Governance options

- **Waterfall**
  - Low risk tolerance
  - Need economies of scale
  - Long service life
  - Less need for innovation
  - Hierarchical culture

- **Hybrids**
  - AgileFall
  - ScrumBan
  - Wagile
  - LeanBan
  - ScrumBut
  - ??

- **Agile**
  - Higher risk tolerance
  - Less need for economies of scale
  - Shorter service life
  - Need for innovation
  - Non-hierarchical culture

> *Orgs may run a waterfall planning phase followed by an agile delivery.*

> *Orgs may run agile projects within the scope of a larger waterfall program. Example: ecommerce within ERP.*

Figure 1-1. The hybrid continuum

While many organizations develop project management practices that mix waterfall and agile, it's important for businesses to understand where they are on the continuum and why.

If you are developing an innovative new product, the more agility your organization can embrace, the more competitive it will be. But for organizations that build power plants or ships, or develop medical technology that lives depend on, there are factors that make a plan-driven approach more appropriate for their projects.

The following factors influence an organization's place on the continuum:

- **Service life** – When the outcomes of an organization's projects have long service lives, plan-driven approaches tend to be the norm. Innovations in endeavors such as shipbuilding, bridge construction, office buildings, and the like do not evolve as rapidly as electronics or computer software.

- **Economies of scale** – A large project that requires significant resources be procured and committed upfront points to a waterfall approach. The construction of a power plant, for example, requires large quantities of concrete and steel be readily available along with a large and reliable workforce. On the other hand, acquiring many developers for a software development project whose requirements are still evolving would be a potentially wasteful decision.

- **Level of risk** – Organizations that need to minimize risks will find themselves operating on the waterfall end of the continuum. For example, the organization that is developing a medical device that impacts life safety must drive risk from the product design and project execution to the extent possible. This factor drives this organization to perform a great deal of planning and research early in the project life cycle to identify and manage risk.

- **Need for innovation** –In contrast to scenarios aimed at minimizing risks, the more the organization can embrace risk and early failures in order to be competitive, the more agile it can be. This flexible approach to project management helps innovative businesses leapfrog competition by getting new versions of product out quickly (whether it's software, hardware, or another physical product), which in turn allows them to implement customer feedback quickly in future iterations.

- **Organizational culture** – Perhaps the most significant influence on an organization's place on the project management continuum is organizational culture. Organizations that are large and bureaucratic tend to find it harder to use agile methods, as this requires quick decisions, direct engagement and feedback, and immediate pivots in response to inputs. More bureaucratic organizations tend to land closer to waterfall on the continuum. With these organizations, it can be difficult to complete quick releases or pivots in strategy when management layers and longer approval processes are part of the culture.

The point of discussing the continuum in agile hybrids is to recognize where your organization sits so that this can be considered in various project management decisions, whether project selection, methodology approach, or likelihood of successful adoption and transition to more agile methods. Organizational placement on the continuum does not necessarily dictate or preclude an approach or predict success or failure of agile implementation. Rather, the continuum helps the practitioner understand the practical realities in play when considering options and making project management decisions at a strategic or tactical level.

Organizations mix their project management strategies based on their endeavors, which is exactly the practical point. I've worked in large enterprise resource planning (ERP) programs in which the overall program was run from a highly plan-driven perspective with a project management office (PMO) in overall control. However, underneath the program level, waterfall and agile projects coexisted with their activities and metrics rolling up to the program layer for overall reporting. In these examples, the ecommerce projects I was responsible for used a highly agile approach underneath the plan-driven program structure.

Hybrid Examples

Hybrid models of project management combine elements of waterfall and agile or combine elements of two agile frameworks. Examples include "AgileFall," "ScrumBan," LeanBan," and "FrAgile" (that's friendly agile). For now, it's important to note that many if not most organizations delivering projects work somewhere in the middle of the continuum noted earlier. It's this middle ground where organizations leverage elements of plan-driven and agile practices that work for their particular culture, business, and scenarios for success on their projects.

Rather than attempt to follow rigid and prescriptive applications of project management methodologies that may not be wholly suited to their cultures or the nature of their business, these organizations are pragmatic and practical. They leverage experienced and well-trained practitioners to combine the most practical and applicable elements of methodologies and frameworks to just get stuff done. In these organizations, the methodology does not matter. As Jesse Fewell states, the methodology is far less important than adapting methodologies to suit the needs and realities of the project and the organization (Fewell, 2010).

The best way to begin learning and thinking about success with agile hybrids is to describe some examples of agile hybrids. One day, I went to do a search on the term "AgileFall." I thought I had created a new term. When I got back thousands of search results for "AgileFall," I realize that many practitioners had long been thinking what I'd been thinking: so many organizations take elements of traditional waterfall practices and combine them with elements of agile. As noted earlier, these hybrids have a lot to do with where the organization is on the continuum.

There are many hybrid examples combining elements of waterfall with agile, or various agile approaches with each other. We will look at a few examples to illustrate how this is done, why it works, and start thinking about how you can evaluate these for use in your organizations and on your projects.

AgileFall

Some agile methodology purists shudder in horror at the idea of AgileFall. Much is written about how to recognize AgileFall as a "bad" thing and what to do about it. The fact is, many organizations find this to be a sweet spot or a comfort zone. AgileFall (or as a former colleague of mine liked to call it "Wagile") is all about balancing elements of agile's flexibility, adaptability, and learning with some degree of predictive planning. There are benefits to both methodologies. Thoughtful and intentional use of elements from both approaches can result in outcomes that might not be as successful if one or the other approach was used in a rigid way.

Organizations working in verticals like consulting, custom product development, software development, and other verticals where some degree of scope definition is necessary can benefit from elements of waterfall in their overall agile approach. As a professional services leader working for the implementation arm of an ecommerce cloud software company, I needed to have some degree of sizing, scope, and requirements discussion with customers upfront. However, the project was defined with latitude built in knowing that as the customer saw deliverables after each sprint, their feedback and experience with the product would lead them to better understand what they really wanted.

This would lead to changes in configuration, deliverables, and completely new ideas for features and functionality. Therefore, an agile approach to the execution and delivery of the project was critical. The AgileFall approach can work well in scenarios like this. A key is forming a partnership with customers early and being very clear about the degree of certainty but also emphasizing how critical the agile and flexible approach with iterative learning and execution is to meeting and satisfying their ultimate requirement.

The approach I took to this AgileFall project and customer partnership was to do the requirements gathering and scoping with the customer to size the approximate duration of the engagement and project. This helped to determine the budget estimate and give the customer some certitude of what they should expect to spend. However, I was very clear in setting expectations with customers. For example, within eight 2-week sprints representing 16 weeks of work, each sprint would reveal changes and inspire customers to think of different ways they would want to adapt or customize the software. The AgileFall approach offered the flexibility to reprioritize features or to add sprints should the customer be interested in increasing their budget and project duration.

ScrumBan

ScrumBan is a hybrid of Scrum and Kanban. Scrum, as we will discuss later in this book, is one of the most widely known and used agile frameworks. In short, it uses predefined and recurring rules, roles, and processes to expedite the release of higher-quality products. One Scrum element is the use of time-boxed iterations or sprints during which teams commit and focus to complete a specified increment of work. There are prescribed meetings – the daily stand-up, the sprint review, and sprint planning meeting (Alexander, 2017). Scrum teams determine the work they will commit to in sprint planning meetings and focus exclusively on completing the work within the sprint, rarely allowing change within the sprint.

Kanban takes its name from the use of a card which is a component in just-in-time manufacturing and delivery. Kanban uses a visual framework to encourage continuous improvement and uses visual workflows to limit work in progress and match desired requirements to a team's ability to deliver. Like Scrum, Kanban relies on self-organizing teams. There are few "formal" roles, and teams meet and change approach or process as needed. Unlike Scrum, Kanban does not generally use time-boxed iterations or sprints as part of the process (Alexander, 2017). Work-in-progress capability is the only limiting factor – there is no prescribed start and end to a period of work.

ScrumBan uses Scrum as an approach to perform the work itself and uses elements of Kanban to seek and realize continuous improvements. ScrumBan can help to maintain focus on managing work in progress, which is a core element of Kanban. While Scrum is often ideal for new product development and Kanban for manufacturing, ScrumBan is useful for maintenance projects and in service verticals where both new development and maintenance work are present (Pahuja, 2017).

ScrumBan combines the Scrum framework and processes with Kanban's process improvement elements and pull process. While Scrum relies on the backlog to manage work and on burndown charts to visualize work completion, ScrumBan focuses on process optimization and smoothing the work-in-process queue. Teams use a board to track work, limit the backlog to a fixed size, and perform planning at regular intervals to prioritize and add items to refill a depleted backlog. Demos and retrospectives may also be performed at regular intervals but are not done at the end of prescribed sprints (Pahuja, 2017).

Estimation in ScrumBan involves planning units of work that fit into the team's work-in-progress queue at approximately the same size, rather than the mix of user stories of varying sizes found in Scrum (more on this later in the book). Estimation is also done as/when needed as opposed to specific points (sprint planning). ScrumBan teams may be specialized (Scrum prefers cross-functional) and may meet daily. ScrumBan allows change to planned work in progress – this differs from Scrum, which generally locks down the sprint commitment for the duration of the sprint.

Savita Pahuja (2017) cites quality, just-in-time fact-finding and decisions, short lead times, continuous improvement, and process improvements as advantages of ScrumBan. Pahuja notes that ScrumBan looks like Scrum at the practice level but like Kanban at a cultural level which can make adoption less jarring and more of an evolution.

Waterfall Plan – Agile Execution

Many organizations seek the security of waterfall planning and a more deliberate approach to project initiation while also seeking the agility and opportunities for incremental and rapid value realization that exist with agile execution. These organizations recognize that there is value in planning, but that the plans themselves are less valuable and, in most projects, will change. They therefore embrace change by executing their planned projects using agile tactics.

The Project Management Institute (PMI) prescribes initiating and planning as the first two phases of what many call a waterfall approach to project management. Organizations that merge waterfall planning with agile execution may perform many project initiation and planning steps including team formation, project infrastructure, communication and stakeholder management planning, and some risk management work.

Organizations that combine these approaches well do not spend too much time trying to define requirements upfront. This is where recognition that projects change and embracing that change helps them realize value from agile execution. These organizations will go into sprints upon launch of their execution phase. They will continuously groom the backlog of original requirements and add or drop features and requirements as the evolving project and input from stakeholders dictate. Even though these organizations did significant planning upfront and may feel they have a good sense of the amount of work and duration of the project, they also recognize that as the project proceeds and they learn more about the output and how the team works, the project duration and overall amount of work required to deliver the desired scope will change.

Organizations using agile execution with waterfall planning can realize rapid value delivery. As the project proceeds through each sprint, the organization can evaluate team accomplishments and determine if completed work is ready to be released or deployed. Rather than waiting until the end to deliver value as with a waterfall execution approach, these organizations use the waterfall planning approach with agile execution to realize incremental value and potentially early project completion.

This approach can also be useful in organizations that are adopting agile but whose leadership may not yet be comfortable with a complete end-to-end agile approach. Retaining elements of waterfall planning helps to provide a degree of comfort to these senior leaders – they see the estimating and risk management elements as particularly useful during project initiation and planning, and also recognize the opportunities for rapid and incremental value realization available through agile execution.

Mixed Environments

Perhaps the most complex situation involving hybrids is an overall hybrid environment mixing waterfall, agile, and hybrid projects in the same project delivery environment within the organization. These organizations will run waterfall projects alongside of agile or hybrid agile projects. This high-level hybrid mixed environment requires significant maturity in project management practices and complete understanding and mastery of each of the methodologies and frameworks that are used.

One of the most challenging parts of the mixed environment is merging the metrics and in some cases dependencies across waterfall and agile projects. Project governance structures must be designed so as to process metrics from all types of projects and synthesize them into actionable information for project governance teams or governance boards.

Projects using different methodologies with cross-project dependencies must have visibility to each other's plans and deliverables. The agile project may negotiate with the waterfall project to ensure that dependent deliverables will be available for sprints based on the respective project plans and release plans for each project.

The challenge in this environment is the likelihood that the waterfall project may have planned completion of a dependent deliverable for the agile team, and then fall behind schedule. The prescriptive plan-driven approach will not likely lend itself to agile replanning so as to deliver the dependent item to the agile team who may have included it in a particular sprint in their release planning.

The benefit here is that the agile team can indeed be agile and update their release plan to pull work from their backlog or restructure their release so as to accommodate the delayed dependent deliverable from the waterfall project.

Case Studies

Let's examine some case studies that illustrate how hybrids and combinations of waterfall and agile methods helped organizations adapt and then adopt new ways of performing projects. In each case, the organization found that elements of agile combined with elements of waterfall were appropriate in some way to achieve their objectives.

Practical Desperation – Trying Agile

I was the project manager on a large, failed, plan-driven ecommerce system replatforming project at a biopharmaceutical company in the mid-2000s. It failed for a few key reasons, the main one being that the vendor underestimated the project and was focused on recovering to profitability through change requests, but also because our leadership had forced the vendor into lowballing their estimate. Fortunately, we had project budget management in place that preserved the majority of our budget when we ultimately parted ways with the vendor and brought the project back in house.

This scenario is not typically where a team would choose to start using some agile practices – the failure of the first edition of this project was highly visible and some of us were surprised to have kept our jobs. However, the project team knew that a plan-driven approach had failed on the first attempt, and that there was too much we did not know about the new technology we were implementing and how the complexity of some of our ecommerce processes would work on this new platform to attempt a plan-driven approach again. We dubbed the project ".NEXT" because we were implementing a Microsoft ecommerce system with a lot of custom development using newest elements of the .NET framework at the time.

The team had minimal formal training or experience with any agile practices, and yet we determined to use Feature-Driven Development (FDD) and to start doing daily stand-ups. We broke the project into its major component features and replanned based on the logical sequence of these feature sets. The iteration lengths varied based on the size of the feature set – some were as short as three weeks, others as long as eight. We determined to demo and release each feature set to end users as soon as it was completed, and we instilled a rigorous and disciplined build and test framework for the development team.

In short, we adopted what was realistic and practical for our team and project scenario at that time. Not everything about this project worked as planned, and we were still several months later than our initial projected completion, but our FDD approach enabled us to tell the business that we were learning as we worked through each feature set and to update our projected completion date after each release. Of equal importance to the team and the organization's further adoption of agile was the learning that took place.

Once this project was completed, the team leveraged its learnings and transitioned into a two-week sprint and release cadence of feature enhancements that lasted for sixteen months. This also set the stage for the organization's continued adoption of agile in incremental and practical ways, examples of which will appear throughout this book.

The Health Insurance Company

I recently spent a year consulting for a large health insurance company. This organization was highly plan-driven and had a large project and program management office (PPMO) with several leaders and many project managers. Their IT department was organized by IT function and was separate from the PPMO. The overall organization was very hierarchical and bureaucratic, and as such they were naturally toward the plan-driven end of the continuum. This organization struggled to get projects done – they approved and launched large technology-driven projects with a great deal of upfront planning on the assumption that massive requirements gathering endeavors would enable them to execute the software development work according to a plan determined by those requirements. These projects were then chronically late and underresourced in critical areas while overstaffed in others.

This organization had failed to recognize that their evolving reliance on software and technology required a move toward the agile end of the continuum. They had, practically speaking, become as much a technology company as a health insurance company. I worked with them as they considered and launched their first agile project and teams, and since I had also worked within their PPMO on some large waterfall projects, I had the perspective to see and recommend changes they needed to make in order to become more efficient and to recognize their evolution into more of a technology-reliant organization.

My recommendation to them after a year was to change their overall operating model and their project delivery model to become a more agile organization. I recommended they adopt some practical agile changes. I recommended that they leverage their experienced functional leaders as product owners and pair them with technology teams to identify opportunities to transform and eliminate operational bottlenecks through technology. I recommended that they change their PPMO model and instead embed their project managers with their business functional areas so that they became real business partners instead of project management as a service. Most importantly, I recommended rigor and discipline in considering and launching projects and ruthless prioritization in approving and executing them.

Shortly after I completed my assignment and made my recommendations, this health insurance company reorganized both its PPMO and IT department and hired a firm specializing in Agile transformations. They began the move that I had recommended and continue their move toward the agile side of the continuum.

SAP and Ecommerce in Biopharma and Cement

SAP is one of the largest and best-known ERP systems and is typically implemented using a prescribed, plan-driven approach. Organizations implementing SAP will typically hire a consulting partner with experience in SAP to plan and lead their implementation program. ERP implementation is a significant endeavor for any organization and certainly benefits from a plan-driven approach. However, even with a plan-driven program, organizations will find it practical and necessary to leverage agile practices for projects within the program. I experienced this on two SAP implementations – one for a midwestern US biopharma and the other for a large cement company based in Bangkok, Thailand.

In both instances, the organizations lived on the plan-driven end of the continuum, and their SAP implementation projects were certainly plan-driven endeavors and rightly so. Within these scenarios, the ecommerce programs that I led used, out of practical necessity, agile practices. Aside from the learnings that came from coordinating agile delivery within plan-driven programs, there were two big learning events that came out of each SAP program.

In the biopharma SAP implementation, the SAP program team began to gradually adopt various agile practices until by the final "playback" (the term given to the iterative attempts to test-drive the ERP system), the SAP project team was referring to elements of the playback as "sprints" and doing daily stand-ups in order to discuss the day's plan and identify impediments. This shows how a heavily plan-driven program benefited from practical application of practices typically associated with agile projects.

In the cement company's SAP implementation, their ecommerce system had (for various reasons) been an afterthought, so my software company's system and implementation team were late additions to the overall program. The SAP program was being run by a PMO from one of the largest global consulting firms in the world, and they were using a program pattern that was familiar to me from my previous experience. Upon arrival in Bangkok, the jet-lagged project director and I were summoned to meet with the "CIA," which caused us much consternation until we learned that "CIA" was a Thai acronym for their PMO.

The PMO insisted that we follow their program management approach and begin providing them with project artifacts that aligned with their overall program. My project director and I explained that due to the late addition of our product and team to their program and given that agile was our normal approach to rapid implementation, we would use our approach while aligning with their needs for reporting as best as possible. The success of this approach proved for me beyond all doubt that agile projects can function well within plan-driven programs.

Salesforce

Salesforce tends toward a "waterfall-ish" approach early in their release cycles before accelerating and transitioning to their agile practices as the release gets going (Ayers, 2016). This works because it is practical – the hybrid approach allows organizations like Salesforce to plan to a point where the level of risk and certainty present in the release is acceptable while still acknowledging the certainty of change while using an approach that can respond to change and provide the opportunity for rapid value realization – the hallmark of agile approaches to project management.

Summary

You've learned about the continuum and how most organizations find themselves and their project management methodologies somewhere on that continuum. You've learned a bit about what often influences where an organization and its projects land on that continuum. You've seen some examples of agile hybrids – AgileFall, ScrumBan, waterfall plan/agile execution, and environments where waterfall and agile methods are used concurrently.

The key takeaway from this opening chapter is that rather than using some "pure" version of agile, most organizations are using and succeeding with forms of agile hybrids – taking the best of waterfall and merging it with elements of agile to create methodologies that work for them and their organizations. In direct contradiction to some experts and practitioners who believe that projects and organizations will fail if they do not follow a pure approach, I contend that a practical approach and embracing a hybrid method that works for you and your organization is the best and most realistic way to go.

In the next chapter, we'll look at ways to assess your own organization and your projects by revisiting the continuum. We'll look more closely at the aspects of your organization, its structure and culture, and the type of projects that you do. This will help you understand where your organization and its projects are on the continuum.

The Continuum Revisited

Where are you?

In my experience, the most successful changes to an organization's approach to project management have occurred when a small group of practitioners just decided to go for it. Whether they have used an approach elsewhere and want to bring it to their new organization or have heard about something different and want to try it – the grassroots interest and enthusiasm of a group of people who think they can improve their ways of working cannot be matched as a foundation for success. That's how it was for us at Promega when the .NEXT team decided to try Feature-Driven Development, created a hybrid project management model, and then extended our learning and use of agile as we moved forward.

Sometimes it is a senior management decision to attempt use of a specific, different project management approach on certain projects or within selected parts of an organization. This often involves telling a working team or group that they will start using an Agile approach instead of whatever they have been using, most likely a phase-based or plan-driven approach. This can potentially go well, or could be disastrous, depending on the circumstances. Attempting to use agile on a project for which an agile framework is not a good fit or jamming agile practices into an environment where people are not ready or

© Shawn Belling 2020

S. Belling, *Succeeding with Agile Hybrids*, https://doi.org/10.1007/978-1-4842-6461-4_2

the culture poses challenges are almost certain to result in poor outcomes and a negative view of agile as an approach to project management.

This is where a hybrid approach comes in. Many organizations can successfully transition from a plan-driven to a hybrid project management approach that blends the working elements of existing plan-driven project management with agile practices to provide results that are aligned with that organization's needs and goals. If this is what seems to make sense for you, it is important to approach the experiment in a planful and intentional way. This starts by assessing where your organization is on the continuum.

Where Are You?

In the previous chapter, I discussed the continuum and the concept that most organizations are not operating at one of the extreme ends but rather somewhere along that continuum. I noted how this is the case due to a variety of factors:

> The business the organization is in
>
> Risk tolerance – both due to the business and due to culture or leadership
>
> Organizational culture
>
> Service life of the products or deliverables
>
> Economies of scale
>
> Need for innovation

In order to consider how to help your organization succeed with a hybrid agile approach, it is important to carefully consider where your organization is on the continuum.

To do that, let's look at some example organizations and examine what elements would point to where they would sit on the continuum. We will look at seven companies in very different lines of business and facing very different risk profiles. Each company has a very different culture based on its age and evolution. We will look at these elements and how they influence where they sit on the waterfall to agile continuum (Figure 2-1).

> A 50-year-old family-owned publishing and consulting company – third generation now running the company; transformed from printing and publishing to software and services company. *The original company culture morphed over 50 years from very conservative with a focus on printing and publishing, certainty of outcomes to a more software-oriented and agile product and company culture.*

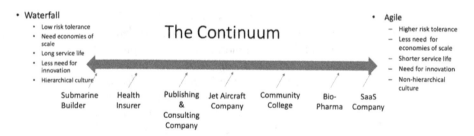

Figure 2-1. Placement of example companies on the Waterfall – Agile Continuum

A 40-year-old global biopharmaceutical research and manufacturing company still led by the founder. *The founder started the company by walking from lab to lab at a major research university selling a reagent to bench scientists. That entrepreneurial spirit created a very flat and informal business culture and still contributes to rapid and sometimes risky product development initiatives.*

A 5-year-old Software-as-a-Service (SaaS) product company having acquired its two biggest customers so far, seeking investors and new customers. *This company is very new, still developing its culture and by necessity incredibly agile. Rapid shifts to their evolving platform and needs of their customers require significant agility in culture and practice.*

A 55-year-old health insurance company, privately held, very traditional and conservative, but realizing its product and IT practices are out of date. *This company reached an epiphany: it recognized that it is as much a technology company as an insurance company. It realized it needed to leverage its best people and technology to evolve and grow their business, and so changed their project model and organizational model to try to become "more agile."*

A 100-year-old community college transforming its student experience with new business processes and technology. *This academic institution adopted a product-oriented mindset to change business process and implement technology with more organizational agility than they have ever experienced. They adopted agile and ongoing release methodology to deliver regular and incremental business value and student-facing features.*

A 130-year-old builder of submarines for the US Navy and other navies around the world. *There is no tolerance for risk when building a submarine that must function under the pressure of the ocean 1000 feet below the surface. Submarines are in service for many decades, and the basic structural design of submarines does not change significantly over these decades. Because of the military connection, there is a strong hierarchical command-and-control culture in place by necessity.*

A 90-year-old Scandinavian builder of jet fighter aircraft. *Perhaps against typical assumptions of an aircraft manufacturer, this company uses scaled scrum to improve and deliver a better aircraft design every six months, and its base fighter is considered the most cost-effective military aircraft. This is an interesting balance of economies of scale and long service life against a need for innovation and some tolerance for risk if it results in a better product and overall program cost management.*

Assessing Projects

There are several things to consider when you are evaluating the types of projects your organizations typically perform and how they help to determine where you are on the continuum. Let's look at some examples and characteristics of projects that are representative of the ends of the continuum.

First, let's consider the project environment that is generally predictable: the projects yield deliverables literally or figuratively built in concrete, brick, steel, glass – things are going to be built once and then remain the same for a very long period of time – deliverables with a long service life, like a building, a ship, or a power plant, or implementing a major software system such as enterprise resource planning (ERP) or electronic medical records (EMR).

With projects like these, objectives tend to be stationary – we know what it is we are trying to achieve at the outset and then we know that target is not going to change. In fact, in these scenarios, change is not desirable once the project is underway, and allowing change in the context of the project could be damaging. We have to consider project planning the way one would consider firing a bullet from a rifle – once we fire the bullet, we are not going to be able to guide it on a trajectory – we have to be certain when we fire that we are on target, so we take time and aim carefully.

This means we seek lots of strategic input at the very start of the project. This contributes to a highly detailed plan to enable us to hit that stationary target. In projects that are suitable for a plan-driven or waterfall approach, we generally gain economies of scale on larger projects, and we get economy of scale as we release large increments of the project. We have a strong emphasis on control, on managing all the outcomes, on trying to stick to the plan and assessing our progress and adjusting to closely follow that plan to achieve our goals.

Now, let's consider a very different project environment. In this environment, project outcomes may be difficult to predict because rapid change is the norm, as is often the case in an environment like technology startups, software development, ecommerce, mobile gaming, life-science research, or new product development. In this environment, the targets are usually moving. Change is good, and the impacts of resisting change could be damaging to the outcome of the project.

Once the work is started, the assumption is that we can guide our work, much like one can steer a guided missile in flight. You launch the missile, you launch the work, and then you can make course corrections to ensure that you hit the moving target or achieve the desired outcome. We seek strategic input throughout the entire project life cycle – it's not something that is provided upfront and then fixed, but rather input we seek constantly to ensure that we are on the right track.

Rapid feedback enables us to stay close to hitting the moving target (like a gazelle being chased by a cheetah) that represents the strategic objectives of a project. We can keep the outcomes relevant and on the moving target by doing rapid, iterative releases so that value can be assessed and aligned with evolving strategic objectives. We use adaptation to achieve our goals and therefore we give up some degree of control in favor of that adaptation. Figure 2-2 illustrates the waterfall or agile aspects of projects.

Environment is predictable; stability is norm; concrete/steel/glass – same for decades = waterfall	Environment difficult to predict; rapid change is norm. High-tech; weekly change = agile > Scrum?
Stationary targets	Moving targets
Change is bad; allowing it is damaging	Change is good, resisting change is damaging
Work directable, like a bullet – aim, aim, fire	Work is guidable like a missile in flight – course corrections, aim, fire, aim
Strategic input needed at start	Strategic input needed throughout
Detailed plan – stationary target	Rapid feedback – moving target
Gain economies of scale with size	Achieve relevance with quick iterative releases
Emphasis on control to achieve goals	Emphasis on adaptation to achieve goals – give up some control

Figure 2-2. Waterfall or agile aspects of projects – (Collyer, Warren, Helmsley & Stevens, 2010, p. 108)

Assessing the Organization

When I began teaching agile project management in 2011, a question that I asked in class was "is your organization ready to adopt agile as a project management approach?". As I write in 2020, it's more appropriate to ask, "why wouldn't your organization be ready to become more agile?" Throughout the 2010s, *Harvard Business Review* (HBR) published a series of articles on agile practices in business (HBR is where Scrum first appeared in Takeuchi and Nonaka's article in 1986). These articles (many coauthored by Jeff Sutherland as well as Hirohito Takeuchi) examined the increasing adoption of agile practices and discussed both cautionary perspectives and advocating for the adoption of agile practices. The new buzz phrase that I see everywhere is "organizational agility" (*as I was drafting this chapter, I literally got an email with this as the subject line*).

Agile and hybrid agile methodologies have moved out of new product development and software development into many other verticals and organizational types. Organizations as diverse as John Deere (farming equipment), National Public Radio (public radio), Saab (fighter jets), and a well-known winery are just a few examples of organizations that have adopted agile practices in some form (some as hybrids) to improve their management and operations and get people out of their functional silos and into new and different ways of thinking (Rigby, Sutherland & Takeuchi, 2016).

It is critical to assess whether your organization is in a good position to make the transition to an agile project management approach or to a hybrid agile approach. There are a number of areas that should be considered and evaluated as you consider introducing a new approach to project management. A thorough, honest, and realistic appraisal of your organization can give you a sense of the size of the hill you are about to climb.

Start by considering your organizational culture. Culture is a complex and multilayered element in this discussion, but one important and obvious consideration is the culture's willingness to accept or tolerate change. Change is never easy, but organizations with a culture that is especially resistant to change, or that has had difficulty with change in the past, may find adoption of agile or hybrid approaches to project management especially difficult.

Organizations that operate in highly regulated industries may find "full" agile does not suit or support their other processes or provide a level of comfort comparable to plan-driven project management approaches. That said, there are practitioners who have implemented agile in regulated environments with appropriate focus on testing and validation processes. In organizations like these, hybrid approaches can work well, mixing elements of plan-driven and agile project management to achieve desired results.

Multitiered and highly bureaucratic organizations are likely to find adoption of agile more challenging than flatter organizations with less bureaucracy. The constant and generally informal communications processes inherent in agile come more naturally to the flatter organizations that have already streamlined their processes and trimmed or avoided bureaucracies.

Take a hard look at your middle management. As organizations grow and mature, it is common to see the growth of middle management layers. It is quite common to see middle managers develop a tendency to focus on defining and protecting their turf or fiefdoms, and these organizations have to address these problems, ideally before considering a methodology that will expose these types of organizational dysfunctions.

Bureaucracies and middle management fiefdoms sound fairly daunting, but given where I am based (Madison, WI), many of the organizations for whom I have done agile training and coaching are state government agencies and the IT department of our flagship state university, as well as within the large insurance companies that are fixtures around Madison. These organizations decided it was worth the effort to try to adopt agile practices or hybrid agile approaches to improve their project delivery and operational execution.

Critical Success Factors

As with any change initiative, there are critical factors that can help increase the odds that experimentation and adoption of new project management practices can be successful. The support and buy-in of the organization's senior leaders are critical, as with any initiative. Cultivation of respected evangelists in the organization who are willing and able to generate interest and support from peers in the organization will help, as will lining up some smaller projects with which to get some quick wins early in the adoption process.

Once the organization decides to go further with agile or hybrid agile, it is important to plan for and invest in good training. This lays a solid foundation of common practices and brings most of the organization in at the same level. Developing and training internal experts combined with solid externally sourced training helps ensure that the organization is well positioned to implement a new approach, as well as develop good processes to support the implementation.

Tips for Successful Implementation

- Leadership buy-in and support
- Evangelists
- Some small, quick wins – start small, evaluate, adapt
- Good training – common training
- Build good processes

Brian Rabon (n.d.) describes some additional ideas for implementing agile project management. Rabon notes that easing into adoption and being pragmatic in one's approach is key. Rabon notes that not every aspect of a methodology should be dogmatically implemented, because (as noted previously) company history and culture has a significant impact. This is once again where a hybrid approach may be your best option – recognizing the history and culture may preclude full adoption of agile, the hybrid approach could acknowledge these aspects while still bringing desirable benefits. The need to embrace change as part of agile is key – a fundamental part of using agile is accepting change. This does not mean abandoning change management, but rather accepting the more flexible perspective that agile brings to change within projects.

Rabon reinforces servant-leadership as an important element. As we will discuss in future chapters, servant-leadership is key for the scrum master/agile PM and senior leaders working in agile environments. Rabon reminds us that being a project manager in agile means it is about the team, and that command-and-control methods will not work. Lastly, Rabon suggests finding a good project or customer as a candidate for piloting agile practices. The project might be a small, less-visible project, but the customer should be one that is willing and able to be fully engaged in the ongoing involvement needed throughout the agile project life cycle (Rabon, n.d.).

A common practice when trying new ways of doing things is to do so on low-stakes or under the radar projects. That way, those interested in experimenting with a new approach (Linux servers, agile development, remote work, flex hours, etc.) can see what works and doesn't work prior to publicizing their experiment. In this way, a small group of practitioners in an organization can try out some practical elements of agile or a hybrid to see how things work in their setting. As a trainer, consultant, and leader, I encourage and support this practice because I have seen it work multiple times, and because the alternative (doing things the same old way) is increasingly unacceptable even while attempting massive change may be too big of a hill to climb all at once.

Practical Examples

I will refer to my early experiences with hybrid agile approaches at Promega Corporation often in this book. In 2009, a new senior leader (Kari) joined Promega to take on executive oversight of both marketing and IT. Kari had come from a successful career at a regional consulting firm where she grew the business by implementing ecommerce projects using agile practices. Joining Promega, she found a small but enthusiastic group of evangelists willing to embrace and grow some of the agile experiments we'd already tried. Kari brought in some trusted consultants and invested in training to help extend the interest and capabilities, and we began to use agile practices more and more – not only on IT projects but on cross-functional marketing/IT projects as well.

At CloudCraze, I joined a small product development team attempting to use agile (Scrum) led by a VP who was also sold on the necessity to use agile for our software development endeavors. Coming in with previous training and experience as well as credibility in that I had begun to teach agile for the University of Wisconsin, the leadership team embraced and supported ongoing learning and adoption of Scrum – not only for product development but for our customer-facing software implementation projects as well.

While consulting for a large health insurance company, I was asked to spin up and lead a web portal enhancement project on which the company wanted to try agile for various reasons. Despite the challenges present in the scenario, the endeavor did have the support of senior leadership. The company also accepted my offer of some short, semiformal agile orientation sessions to generate some basic awareness of agile within the organization. Agile definitely took off there – after I completed my assignment, the company did a major reorganization of their PMO and their IT department and launched an agile transformation program.

Typical Impediments

There are challenges typical to the adoption and implementation of agile in many organizations. It's become widely accepted that rigorous implementation of agile will reveal or highlight problems in other areas – one thing I like to say is that there is nowhere to hide on an agile team, and the same is true in an agile organization.

Often, the challenges are with management or at the organizational level. Many senior leaders think that agile is a quick or magic fix and therefore expect to see the benefits from agile without making real changes in supporting business processes and philosophies. As we discussed in a previous chapter, senior leaders must be part of the change and must in fact be the removers of impediments at the leadership and organizational level.

At the functional level, there are plenty of obstacles as well. Too often, team members, especially those who feel that they don't really need to be in every daily stand-up meeting, find reasons not to attend, and soon the value of their involvement is lost along with the expectation. Along these same lines, the stand-ups themselves may be poorly run, or run in an undisciplined way that diminishes their value and makes people not want to participate.

Team members also may resist some of the other changes in routines that come with best practice implementation of agile, such as co-location and ready accessibility. The collaborative team work and accountability required for successful agile can be an issue for people who see themselves as above their peers. As well, some people just don't want to give up their private offices or other perqs of their positions for the relative equality of an agile team.

Agile and hybrid agile approaches rely on constant direction and involvement from product owners, and many times the people filling this role are, or choose to be, too busy to provide the close engagement and involvement required to be a strong product owner. It may also be that they may not be willing or able to make the tough decisions needed to regularly prioritize a backlog of features that can't all be realized in a single project or release.

Another impediment emerges when managers use the metrics generated in agile to put pressure on the team. For example, instead of using velocity as a measure of sustainable performance and throughput, they pressure the team to work faster or take on larger commitments.

Additional challenges come when one area in an organization such as IT or product development chooses to adopt agile while the remainder of the organization retains other methods for managing projects. Again – this is where a coordinated, hybrid approach that allows flexibility depending on the project type, department needs, and other factors can be the best choice. Earlier, I noted the encouraging trend from the late 2010s into 2020 showing that agility throughout organizations is gaining traction, so hopefully this impediment decreases in frequency.

In software development, a challenge comes in the change of mindset from project-based software delivery to an ongoing, sustained delivery model in which a team can maintain a pace of regular value-adding releases. Generally speaking, the change in mindset from getting all features, benefits, and value all at once at the end of a long project can be a problem for organizations – they cannot adapt to the roadmap approach in which prioritized business value is delivered incrementally and ongoing.

The ownership of the product owner role can be a challenge in some organizations. It requires hard choices and discipline to constantly assess the value of the product backlog and accept that you can have some things now and some things in later releases.

Organizations that see their agile/hybrid agile implementations fail or become muted often experience this because the people attempting to implement the new method ultimately give in to the resistance of the culture and dysfunctional elements. Influential people in the organization, often people who are fearful, resistant, or skeptical of any type of project management, use this influence to undermine the adoption for fear of the change it may effect or out of impatience or lack of appreciation for the value it could bring. The challenges noted here are where an agile coach can be extremely valuable in reminding an organization why they started with a new approach and helping them to assess how to get the adoption and implementation on track.

It's important to ensure that everyone in the organization understands that agile does not equate to immediate faster delivery. It is also important to note that at times, changes identified by the teams may slow them down temporarily. I've offered the advice and observation that teams would need to slow down in order to go faster many times. Tommy Norman, a Lean/Agile coach, notes:

> *Be careful promising your stakeholders that moving to Agile will increase delivery speed right out of the gate. Methods like Scrum and Kanban help to quickly expose issues around delivery, but they don't fix them. When you first adopt Agile, you will be presented with these opportunities to address your issues, but that takes time and experimentation. Initially you might actually be SLOWER until you can address the right issues. If people come into Agile thinking that at the end of your first Sprint there will be some significant increase in productivity, they might be disappointed and start to think Agile is the problem. Set expectations appropriately and help people learn to see the value in exposing and addressing underlying issues. Show them the value in slowing down to speed up.*
> (Norman, 2019)

Summary

We've discussed the importance of understanding where your organization and the type of projects it does sits on the continuum spanning waterfall practices on one end and highly agile practices on the other end. Assessing elements such as culture, risk tolerance, need for scale or innovation, and organizational hierarchy are all important aspects of determining what type of hybrid suits your organization and its projects, and what elements of waterfall and agile you will bring to this hybrid. In Chapter 3, we will discuss how to approach building a hybrid methodology by using the example from an organization where I helped to design, build, and implement a hybrid agile project management methodology that proved to be very successful.

Building Your Agile Hybrid

Getting started — moving forward

The first two chapters of this book have introduced and defined agile hybrids, provided some examples, and given you a framework to assess where your organization and its projects may be on a continuum between full plan-driven project management and very agile project management. This chapter will give you ideas on how to actually build a hybrid agile methodology for your organization. It is important to know from the start that this will be an iterative journey, much like the projects that the methodology is used to deliver. Assume that you will start and build an approach, learn from its application, and continuously refine it — same as what is done in an agile project.

This chapter will discuss building a hybrid methodology by using examples from some scenarios that I've personally led or participated in. In these examples, the organization had an existing project management methodology, whether phase-based, plan-driven, or even a nascent attempt at agile. As each organization evolved and started to become interested in using agile practices in its project delivery, the methodology evolved to become a hybrid,

© Shawn Belling 2020
S. Belling, *Succeeding with Agile Hybrids*, https://doi.org/10.1007/978-1-4842-6461-4_3

or in some cases an umbrella that enabled use of both plan-driven and agile practices within the same program.

■ **Note** Developing and improving a hybrid agile project management methodology is a journey – an iterative process. Same as with agile projects – learn from use, iterate, and improve.

What Do You Know?

The first two chapters have shown you how to assess your organization and determine what you know about its culture, structure, and the types of projects typically run within your organization. This self-knowledge about your organization is critical to designing a hybrid agile methodology that is suited to your organization and its projects. Using the tools and examples introduced in Chapters 1 and 2, it is important for you and your team, stakeholders and sponsors, other influential people in the organization, to take the time to assess the organization and confirm where you are and who you are. Forming a solid foundational consensus of the organization and its project management needs is critical to developing the first version of your hybrid agile methodology.

In this case, "what do you know?" is intended to get you thinking about these cultural and process elements already in place. The following examples will demonstrate what I mean by this and hopefully give you some patterns and ideas on how you can have these conversations yourself within your organization.

Example – Technology Consulting Firm

In 2012 I joined a technology consulting firm as a principal consultant and project management competency lead. The firm had three lines of business: ecommerce, something called CPQ (Configure, Price, Quote), and a Salesforce implementation practice. When asked to update the project management and proposal estimating and development processes, I assessed the organization's culture and the types of projects we typically delivered. Given aspects of the systems we were usually implementing and the customers we worked with, it was clear we needed to evolve from the highly plan-driven, phase-based project management approach that was in place. This change would help us be a more nimble delivery organization and accelerate our growth, especially in our ecommerce business where we had developed a revolutionary new software-as-a-service (SaaS) product that could be implemented very rapidly. We knew a couple of key things: our customers were beginning to adopt agile practices, and we needed to be able to ramp up our projects quickly and begin delivery without an extended planning phase.

Example – Biopharma Company

At the biopharmaceutical company where I was one of several IT project managers, the gradual adoption of agile after it was used to deliver a major ecommerce replatforming was gaining traction. Our IT leadership and a new senior director over marketing and IT were increasingly interested in adopting and leveraging agile practices.

However, we all knew the rest of the organization was just beginning to embrace more familiar phase-based, plan-driven project management. We knew that a sudden pivot to agile would have been very jarring and confusing – it would need to be socialized and introduced as complementary to the existing project management processes.

Example – State Investment Board

A couple of years prior to writing this book, I did some consulting work for a state investment board. This organization manages the investments behind my state's retirement system. This organization wanted to leverage more agile practices in the development and delivery of its IT systems.

Early in the process, I spent time working with the person advocating for agile. It is important to keep in mind that investing, particularly when you are responsible for the retirement funds of an entire state workforce, is a historically risk-averse culture. The sponsor knew that this aversion to risk permeated the organizational culture. He also knew that most of the people there had spent their career using waterfall project management practices, and so relating agile practices back to their corollary in waterfall practices would help make things more relatable.

It also helped us as we talked with influential sponsors and stakeholders to tell them that while agile adoption was not mandatory, understanding where they should focus their energy, where they could get the most value, and where they would impede the agile adoption if they did not adopt certain practices were all important factors for them to understand.

Example – Marketing Software Company

In 2017, I was working as vice president of software development for a cloud ecommerce company. As part of my job, I spent time talking to other leaders of development at similar companies to learn more about their practices and what was working for them. One of these leaders (Herry) shared how when he first joined his organization, he learned that they had a very slow organizational culture with three big software teams and an old code base. His charge was to speed up and scale up the development process.

His assessment helped him determine how to change the project management methodology to a hybrid of Lean and Kanban, with a focus on attaining flow. This leader also recognized that he needed to change the culture in team leadership and accountability. For this hybrid methodology to work, it was important to instill a culture of shared accountability for the completion and delivery of quality software, where everyone owned quality – not just the QA team.

What Do You Have?

The project management body of knowledge, or PMBOK, often refers to what are called "process assets." "Process assets" is just a fancy name for tools, processes, and templates that your organization already has in place. These process assets may be existing project management processes, tools, and templates, or they may be other business process tools and templates.

Depending on your organization and its existing maturity in project management, there may be process assets in place that have been used successfully and can be adapted or serve as foundations for an evolving agile hybrid methodology. It is not necessary to "reinvent the wheel" if any of these elements are working, are familiar to others in the organization, and if their use has been adopted widely throughout the organization.

Example – The Biopharma Corporation

The biopharma had a set of existing project management templates that were widely used, fine-tuned, and familiar to many people in the organization from their use on five years of previous projects. As our hybrid agile methodology evolved, these templates were adapted to reflect the increased use of agile practices. Where appropriate, new templates were created to capture artifacts such as user stories. Familiar aspects of the template were retained, while new elements to reflect agile practices and artifacts were added or created.

A good example is the document used for project request and initiation. Rather than create a new document to initiate projects that were flagged as likely to be run using agile practices, we retained the existing project charter. Certain elements of the charter were tweaked to reflect that fewer elements of the project were known or identified at this early stage and would be refined as the project moved forward.

Another example is the introduction of a release plan template. The existing phase-based methodology had a document intended for use in documenting the narrative of the project plan. This document was augmented with a release plan template. It showed how deliverables would initially be slotted within sprints in the release plan. It also noted specifically that it was a dynamic document that would be updated after each release.

Example – Technical Consulting Firm

The consulting firm had process assets from its first attempt at creating its own branded approach to project delivery. (For some reason, consulting firms that use projects to deliver value to clients feel compelled to create their own branded approach to project management.) I determined that some of these could be adapted to a hybrid agile methodology.

For example, the template used to create proposals also served a number of project initiation and definition purposes. The proposal also ultimately served as the document in which the final detailed project plan was conveyed. When the revised proposal template was combined with the revised estimating process and templates that used the projected duration of the project along with the planned size of the team, it was fairly easy to create a hybrid proposal and planning template to add to the existing plan-driven process assets.

Example – Marketing Software Company

Herry, the head of development at the marketing software company, had a solid quality assurance team in place – they had existing testing practices and tools, and a strong leader. The problem was that this team was also a bottleneck due to the way the overall organization operated. Leveraging the existing process assets of QA combined with the hybrid of Lean and Kanban helped Herry eliminate QA as a bottleneck and instead leverage QA as an asset. Herry also created a culture of shared responsibility for quality and the QA process baked into the new hybrid project management methodology.

What Do You Need?

The question "what do you need" is driven by the answers to some of the other questions asked in this chapter as well as many other factors. It comes down to what kind of projects you deliver and expect to deliver with the hybrid approach. Taking the time to assess the current state of project management may very well reveal that there are missing processes or templates that are needed to be effective independent of creating and implementing a hybrid agile methodology.

This assessment could be an opportunity to not only work on developing your hybrid but also to shore up gaps and deficiencies in your existing (and perhaps successful) project management methodology. Remember, you are not interested in doing away with anything that has been successful for the organization. You are interested in creating an additional approach to project management that will be beneficial to the organization and introduce needed agility.

Although some agile purists may advocate doing away with the essential elements of traditional project management, the experienced and pragmatic practitioner finds that these elements are still present in agile, although applied in different ways and at different points and cadences throughout a project life cycle. As you assess and answer the question "what do you need," consider elements such as stakeholder communications, risk management, project initiation, charters, procurement processes, and other traditional project management artifacts. You will need some form of these in your hybrid approach, or you may simply adapt and adopt them with the modifications necessary to enable desired agility and flexibility within project delivery.

Example – Technical Consulting Firm

The technical consulting firm needed a defined and disciplined agile process that would incorporate the realities of consulting work while retaining the flexibility of agile delivery. By this I mean that clients wanted a cost and duration estimate prior to signing a statement of work document – a reasonable expectation. They also wanted to be "agile" – essentially, they wanted things both ways. Our estimating and statement of work documents became the instruments for documenting and communicating our agile practices to the client while also providing a vehicle for the client and our firm to negotiate and manage agile change.

Example – Biopharma Corporation

The head of IT at the biopharma had a clear vision in mind for what was needed as a hybrid methodology. His exact words were "lightweight, rapid, managed." This need was defined by an interest in ensuring that waterfall and agile project management did not become, or become perceived as, too process-heavy. He also wanted to convey that projects would move through the project management process and life cycle rapidly while being appropriately managed.

Example – A Technical College

When I became the CIO of a large midwestern technical college, I encountered a project management process that was extremely and unnecessarily complex – so much so that people in the college did everything they could to circumvent the process. It was clear to me that a much simpler approach to assessing and initiating projects that stressed conversations and partnership versus process and documentation was needed. I sensed that the people and culture of the college would respond much better to an approach that clearly valued relationships and collaboration over process and detailed initiation paperwork.

Who Do You Need?

The question "who do you need" is driven by your organizational culture. You will need a strong sponsor for this endeavor. As stated earlier, this is true of any organizational change, but perhaps even more so with a new approach to project management. You will also need the buy-in of influential people in the organization, especially those who will use or interact with your evolving hybrid agile project methodology. The people who will be most affected by changes to project management methodology should be involved and of course bought into the process of developing and implementing a hybrid agile approach to project management.

Example – Biopharma Company

Kari had joined the biopharma as the senior director overseeing marketing and IT. She had previously been a vice president at a successful technical consulting firm where she used hybrid agile practices to grow the business and deliver widely recognized successful projects. Coming into the biopharma, her interest and strong sponsorship for developing and adopting hybrid agile practices was not only critical to adoption, it helped to add momentum to some grassroots work that had already been started.

The grassroots work to developing more agile practices and weaving them into the traditional project management approach was crucial to the success of the hybrid agile approach. Because influential managers and practitioners were already on board, this combined momentum helped to accelerate the development and adoption.

Example – Technical Consulting Firm

The founder and CEO of the consulting firm was keenly interested in evolving project management practices to reflect the interests of our clients in using more agile approaches to project delivery. The more we worked with clients interested in rapid adoption of our new ecommerce system, the clearer it became that the older plan-driven approach needed to evolve to a hybrid approach with many elements of agile as core to the new methodology.

The CEO's support was critical, but equally critical was the buy-in from other principal consultants as well as the business development team. The principal consultants, architects, project managers, and business development staff were the people who would need to estimate, plan, sell, and ultimately deliver using this new hybrid approach. Without their support, this effort would have gone nowhere.

Where Do You Start?

Implementing change in any organization for any reason can be a daunting prospect. If an organization has been using a project management methodology with some success (or without success but with familiarity) for a long time, pushing for change will encounter resistance. We will discuss agile implementation in more detail later in this book. For now, it is important to know that two important places to start in this endeavor are evangelism and training.

Evangelism – Getting a group of influential people to believe and to start socializing the change and the need for change is important to creating awareness of the need to change. Then they can start getting people thinking and talking about adopting and adapting new project management methods. Evangelism of the need to change and of the new way for doing things is not unique to adopting new project management practices; this is true about any important organizational change.

The other critical place to start is with a common basis in training. Later in this book, we talk about adopting agile project management practices, and we note that a common basis in training is critical to successful adoption. When starting your hybrid agile methodology, it is important that you start thinking about how you will develop and deliver the training. You are likely to be developing something that is unique to your organization and your needs, so off-the-shelf training may not exist. An experienced consultant may be able to help you outline ideas for your hybrid methodology as well as how to develop and deliver the training needed.

Example – Financial Insurance Company

I did some work for an insurance company that specializes in mortgage loan insurance. This organization wanted to ensure that their people who have a more casual relationship with project management understood both waterfall and agile project management methods as well as how these could be blended and used in a hybrid approach. The mortgage insurance company started by creating a common basis in training for a cohort of team leads whose main jobs did not always involve project management, but who needed to have an awareness of project management to be effective leaders and to occasionally manage small projects themselves.

Building from this initial awareness, the company used its extensive training capabilities to guide people to additional project management training appropriate to their roles and to their interests in learning more about project management, whether agile or plan-driven.

Example – Biopharma

At the biopharma company, we began to evangelize the use of agile alongside of, mixed with, or in place of the existing plan-driven practices. This evangelism was supported because a cohort of us had been successful with a hybrid agile project delivery and wanted to ensure others knew how we had done this and how it could be repeated on future projects. Our new senior director was an advocate of hybrid agile herself and had also brought along people she had worked with elsewhere to advocate for more agile approaches to delivering projects.

I was assigned to find or create the training programs for IT and software development that emphasized iterative development as well as emerging agile practices. IT and marketing management were bought into the idea of establishing this common basis in training to help ensure projects using hybrid methodologies would be more successful because the team members and sponsors and functional managers would all be working from the same basis in training. We ended up writing some of our own training (which subsequently became the foundation of an agile course I taught at the University of Wisconsin for nine years) as well as bringing in some local and national talent to provide training on specific agile topics.

What Next?

Chapter 3 has been focused on helping you think about building a hybrid agile approach to project management. We've helped you assess your organization thinking about what you know about your culture, people, and projects. We've helped you determine how to assess what you already have that will help you get started. We've looked at what you will need and whose support you will need in order to be successful, and we've talked about ways to get started.

The title of this book is *Succeeding with Agile Hybrids*, and the keyword here is "agile." For this reason, the second part of this book will focus on learning agile. "Agile" is the foundation for hybrid agile approaches to project management as espoused in the book. Chapter 4 will discuss the history of agile, examining its origins and how it evolved over decades to become the popular and widely used set of methodologies today.

Chapters 5 through 9 will discuss the core elements of agile methodologies, teams, agile leaders, and the role of agile coaches. Chapters 10, 11, and 12 will explore more advanced topics in agile such as design thinking, the role of the executive leader, and some approaches to scaling agile. Taken as a foundational discussion of how to be successful with hybrid agile methodologies combined with the foundation in good agile practices, you will be well positioned to lead in your organization as hybrid agile evangelist and practitioner.

Learning Agile

Agile History

Roots of Agile

As we begin discussing the practical application of agile, it's important to understand where agile came from. Contrary to popular belief, agile practices did not appear in 2001 with the Agile Manifesto (more on this later). Contemporary practice of agile traces its roots to Scrum, which in turn looks back to quality processes in manufacturing and evolving methods in product development prior to alignment and adaptation for software development and other projects.

> **Note** Agile can be traced back to manufacturing and quality practices pioneered by Ohno at Toyota and the work of quality gurus such as Deming, Shewhart, and Juran.

I like to ask students in my agile project management classes if they own or have ever owned a Toyota automobile (in my case, I've owned three). I ask this because one can trace agile to Taiichi Ohno's Toyota Manufacturing System (TPS) as well as to the work of quality experts such as W. Edwards Deming and Joseph Juran. Following World War II, Japan worked to rebuild its heavy industry and sought the advice of experts such as Deming and Juran, whose work was not gaining much traction in the United States.

At the core of the TPS, other quality systems and methods, and the agile frameworks, there is a common element: the plan-do-check-act (PDCA) cycle

© Shawn Belling 2020

S. Belling, *Succeeding with Agile Hybrids*, https://doi.org/10.1007/978-1-4842-6461-4_4

(Figure 4-1). Typically credited to Deming and variously called the Deming circle or Shewhart cycle, the PDCA cycle is at the heart of most agile frameworks and can help the practitioner remember the essence of the approach (Moen & Norman, 2010).

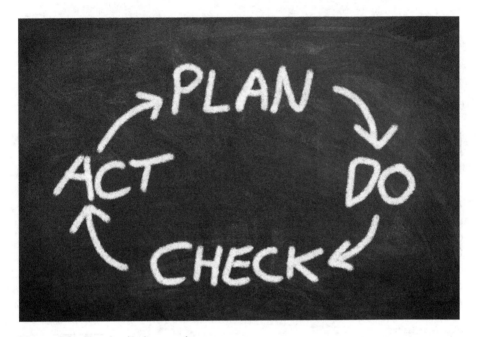

Figure 4-1. Plan-do-check-act cycle

When at any point it becomes necessary for a practical reminder of what agile is about, remember PDCA. Agile is much more than this, but PDCA helps focus teams on how to execute.

Roots of Agile Frameworks: Scrum

When thinking about agile from a practical perspective, it is critical to understand that many well-known agile practices are derived from Scrum. Jeff Sutherland is widely known in agile circles as the co-creator of Scrum and its most passionate advocate and practitioner. Sutherland credits the work of Hirotaka Takeuchi and Ikujiro Nonaka and their 1986 article in the *Harvard Business Review* as foundational to the creation and evolution of Scrum (Sutherland, 2011). In their seminal 1986 article, Takeuchi and Nonaka illustrate the distinction and advantages of a rugby-like approach to new product development versus the traditional relay race approach. The article introduces the word "scrum" and makes a direct comparison to the rugby scrum to describe the approach to new product development that evolved to become one of the roots of the Scrum framework and ultimately most agile frameworks (Takeuchi and Nonaka, 1986).

While the article itself is dated, the core concepts of Scrum and agile are present in the work of Takeuchi and Nonaka and resonate as clearly today as they did when first written. Takeuchi and Nonaka describe six principles that all agile practitioners should be familiar with:

1. Built-in instability
2. Self-organizing project teams
3. Overlapping development phases
4. "Multilearning"
5. Subtle control
6. Organizational transfer of learning

Takeuchi and Nonaka state that "These characteristics are like pieces of a jigsaw puzzle. Each element, by itself, does not bring about speed and flexibility. But taken as a whole, the characteristics can produce a powerful new set of dynamics that will make a difference" (Takeuchi and Nonaka, 1986).

Jeff Sutherland defined the initial Scrum rules, the meetings that are inherent to the Scrum methodology, and the artifacts that are used within Scrum. Working with Ken Schwaber, Sutherland presented this methodology at a software development conference in 1995. The paper described and introduced the Scrum method. These writings formalized and documented an approach to software development that could be adapted and improved upon going forward.

Formation and Emergence

Other approaches to software development continued to develop throughout the mid-1990s. Kent Beck, another influential agile figure, came up with the concept of Extreme Programming, often abbreviated as XP, in 1996. Beck focused on frequent releases of software and short development cycles. One key element is the use of paired programming, where software developers work closely together with one at the keyboard and another looking over the shoulder or sitting side by side – literally two sets of eyes looking at the code and collaborating in real time, as the best way to actually write and implement a feature.

Kent Beck was also instrumental in another approach to agile development that is known as Test-Driven Development (TDD). There is a focus on short development cycles, but one of the key points here is that a software developer would start with the test itself. They would write a failing test for a particular feature, and then they would write code until that code would pass the test.

Closely related to this concept is Feature-Driven Development (FDD), which was pioneered by Jeff De Luca in 1997. The project would be driven from a list of requirements and tasks from a feature list. The project team would build an overall model or design, and then the project would be planned feature by feature. The team would design each feature, and each feature would be built out and tested — so the process of working through each feature design, build, and test is essentially what would drive the project.

Kanban and Lean

Kanban emerged in the 1940s from the work of Toyota and their manufacturing system. It is said that Toyota observed how grocery stores replenish their shelves, basing replenishment on the stock on the shelves vs. the supply that their vendors wanted them to take. We see this manifest as management of work in progress.

In Kanban, we only pull in more work when there is "space on the shelf" so to speak. This is often what is called the "just-in-time" approach to manufacturing for inventory or to providing work in progress. "Kanban" itself refers specifically to a visual signal or card. At Toyota, this card appeared in a basket of parts to indicate that it is time to send the card back up stream so that more parts can be released into the manufacturing workflow.

Kanban was adopted in many manufacturing and service work settings, and in the early 2000s, some began to adopt Kanban practices for the management of knowledge work (Terry, 2018).

As with Kanban, Lean has roots that trace back to automobile manufacturing. Some look all the way back to Henry Ford's production line. There is solid evidence that Toyota and the Toyota Production System perfected lean principles to make their manufacturing processes more efficient by ensuring that the process stops when there is a defect. Human observation is critical to ensure that defects are detected and that production stops until the reason for the defect is addressed and fixed (Skhmot, 2017).

One source for the emergence of lean principles in manufacturing is a 1991 book by James Womack, Daniel Jones, and Daniel Roos in which the authors studied various manufacturing systems and compared them to the methods in place at Toyota.

Lean principles trace value from the customer perspective and seek to illuminate any steps in production that do not create value. Lean seeks to streamline processes so that product and value flows toward the customer and allows customers to pull their value from the next activity. Constant attention to the value stream ensures that any waste is removed, and that flow and pull are enhanced with the intention of creating a perfect value stream (Skhmot, 2017).

2001 – The Manifesto

One of the key events in the adoption of Agile, particularly in software development, comes in early 2001. A group of early agile thinkers and practitioners met in Snowbird, Utah, and they memorialized a set of values known as the Agile Manifesto (Figure 4-2). Note that they did not discard the items on the right or indicate that they were of no value, but rather placed higher value on the items on the left.

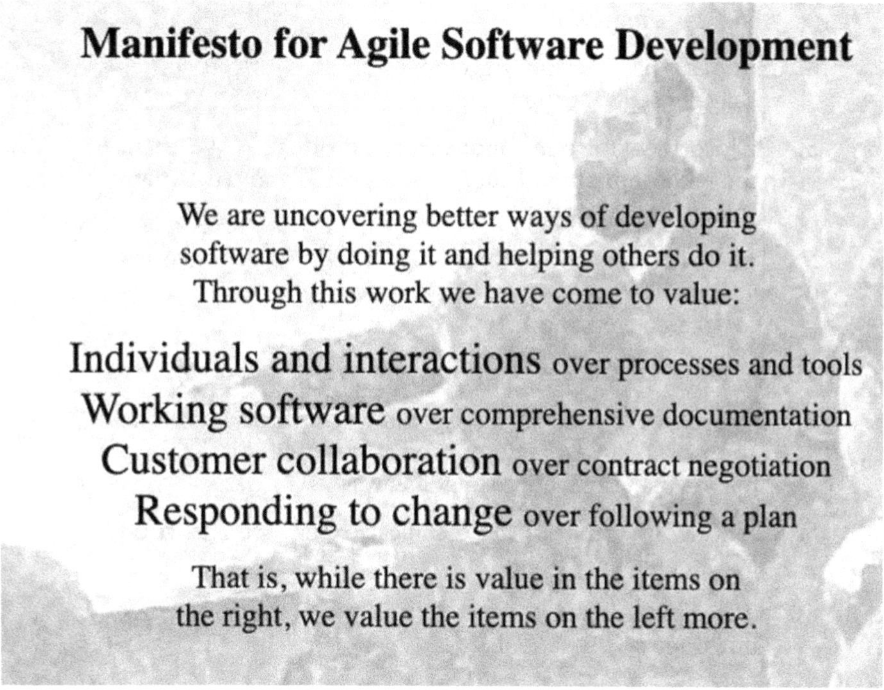

Manifesto for Agile Software Development

We are uncovering better ways of developing software by doing it and helping others do it. Through this work we have come to value:

Individuals and interactions over processes and tools
Working software over comprehensive documentation
Customer collaboration over contract negotiation
Responding to change over following a plan

That is, while there is value in the items on the right, we value the items on the left more.

Figure 4-2. The Agile Manifesto (agilemanifesto.org, 2001)

The most critical thing with the Agile Manifesto as it applies to practical agile is to embrace and live these key values. As Dr. Jeff Sutherland notes, "Agile is not a process, it is a set of values" (Sutherland, 2019). In addition to PDCA, keeping the Agile Manifesto values at the forefront of practice is key to practical agile delivery. In addition to the Manifesto itself, the collaborators developed twelve principles behind the Agile Manifesto which provide the foundations for the agile frameworks and practices you may already be familiar with and which are discussed in this book.

It is important to understand the twelve principles to fully comprehend the Manifesto. It is also important to keep in mind that, though the Manifesto authors were coming at this from a software development perspective, if you replace the word "software" with "product," and it helps to broaden the context and application of these principles.

1. Our highest priority is to satisfy the customer through early and continuous delivery of valuable software.

2. Welcome changing requirements, even late in development. Agile processes harness change for the customer's competitive advantage.

3. Deliver working software frequently, from a couple of weeks to a couple of months, with a preference to the shorter timescale.

4. Business people and developers must work together daily throughout the project.

5. Build projects around motivated individuals. Give them the environment and support they need and trust them to get the job done.

6. The most efficient and effective method of conveying information to and within a development team is face-to-face conversation.

7. Working software is the primary measure of progress.

8. Agile processes promote sustainable development. The sponsors, developers, and users should be able to maintain a constant pace indefinitely.

9. Continuous attention to technical excellence and good design enhances agility.

10. Simplicity – the art of maximizing the amount of work not done – is essential.

11. The best architectures, requirements, and designs emerge from self-organizing teams.

12. At regular intervals, the team reflects on how to become more effective and then tunes and adjusts its behavior accordingly (agilemanifesto.org, n.d.).

Following 2001 and the emergence of the Agile Manifesto, agile methods and practices experienced accelerating adoption within software development and also in other domains and verticals interested in adopting agile project management processes and techniques and methodologies for their use.

2010–2020

Prior to 2010, the Project Management Institute (PMI) and its core certification of Project Management Professional (PMP) were perceived such that many practitioners of agile said "we don't want to be like them." In turn, PMI and many practitioners of PMI's project management body of knowledge (PMBOK) believed that agile methods lacked rigor and discipline and were not robust or mature enough for critical projects. Yet in 2010, PMI recognized agile as a viable method of managing projects and announced its own certification in agile, the PMI Certified Agile Practitioner (PMI-ACP).

PMI's embrace of agile was the essence of practicality. In addition to recognizing that aspects of agile had been around for decades (rolling wave project planning being one example), PMI also recognized that agile was gaining significant traction and that it would be much better (and profitable) to embrace agile. Within PMI's practitioner ranks, people like Jesse Fewell were advocating a pragmatic view of agile as a complementary approach to managing projects that had its appropriate place in the spectrum and toolkit of organizations and project managers.

The years 2010–2020 also saw the proliferation of training, additional flavors of agile certifications, the emergence and acquisition of entire methodologies (e.g., Disciplined Agile, which was acquired in 2019 by PMI), and continued consternation on the part of agile purists who (with some reason) decry the dilution of the core values of agile. As a practitioner, writer, and teacher, I've observed this expansion and dilution and see it as all the more reason to focus on hybrid and practical approaches and outcomes that leverage the basic tenets of agile.

The 2010s saw recognition from adopters that agile could not automatically solve systemic problems. The 2010s saw the emergence of mixing and adapting to create the hybrid approaches which are the focus of this book: A departure from orthodoxy and purist approaches in agile project management, replaced by a trend of taking the elements that work best while adapting or discarding other elements that may not work for particular projects and organizations.

This mixing and adapting of hybrid approaches, taking elements that work best while adapting or discarding other elements that may not work for particular projects and organizations, is our focus: The recognition that while agile frameworks like Scrum provide their best and most impactful results when deeply understood and implemented to their purest and fullest extent, there are unquestionably benefits from understanding and applying elements of agile frameworks that work for practitioners and their organizations while recognizing that not all organizations can (or should) worry about doing a "perfect" implementation of an agile framework.

Summary

In Chapter 4, we learned a bit about the roots and history of agile – where it came from, how it evolved where it was used, and how it emerged to become the set of frameworks that we are becoming familiar with and that have been widely adopted. This is important because this helps you understand key elements that should always be present in your application of the frameworks, tools, and techniques, regardless of whether you are using a hybrid or a purist approach.

Chapter 5 will discuss more agile values such as flexibility and adaptability before diving into the agile life cycle and practices.

Agile Values and Practices

Beyond the Manifesto

I often start my agile project management classes by asking students what they think of when they read or hear "agile" (I always think of a cheetah). Students typically respond with "fast, nimble, flexible, responsive." I mention the cheetah in the context of chasing a gazelle: The cheetah's goal is the gazelle, which is constantly moving and changing direction – much like the requirements and objectives of some projects. The cheetah must process the input of the gazelle's changes in direction along with the changes in the landscape and respond to these changes in order to accomplish the goal of catching the gazelle.

Agile project management describes a set of methods and techniques that help project teams and organizations do the same thing: go fast and be responsive to change. In practice, agile methods are often blended with plan-driven approaches and other agile methods into hybrid approaches. These hybrid approaches are adapted to fit the culture of the organization, its structure, and its appetite for risk and change.

Agile methods are iterative, adaptive, and interactive and place a premium on teams and teamwork. In agile, teams are self-managed while accountable for

© Shawn Belling 2020
S. Belling, *Succeeding with Agile Hybrids*, https://doi.org/10.1007/978-1-4842-6461-4_5

delivering value regularly and frequently. Most agile frameworks use short, time-boxed iterations of focused work, often called sprints, during which constant communication within the team and with stakeholders ensures the team works on the right things toward the right outcomes.

Note In practice, most organizations blend plan-driven approaches with agile practices to create their own hybrid approach – the focus of this book.

Agile Life Cycle Models

Let's look at a basic agile project life cycle. Regardless of plan-driven or agile approaches, projects start with the vision of something that the performing organization wants to have. I like to show Stephen Thomas' agile life cycle (Figure 5-1). Thomas' model illustrates the hybrid approach with the pre-project planning and then initiation phase of the project. There is team formation, development of an initial plan, development and documentation of some initial requirements (backlog), and the setup of any infrastructure needed in order to perform the project work. In this model, a waterfall planning approach is performed prior to moving into the agile sprint execution phase.

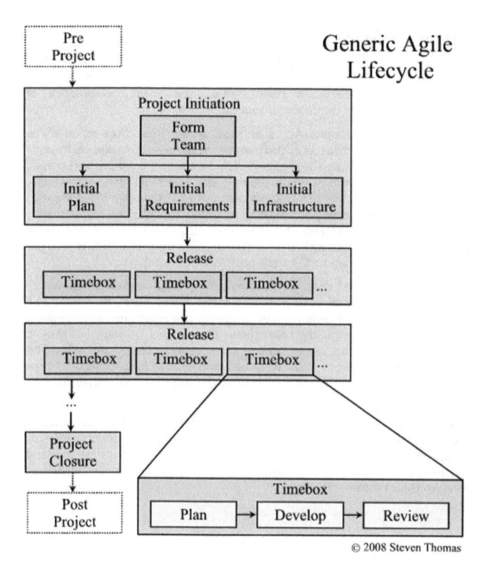

Figure 5-1. Hybrid agile life cycle (Thomas, 2008)

Thomas' model shows how each time box (iteration) has some planning work, development work, and a review (plan-do-check-act). The work is planned, the team commits to the work, the team performs the work, and the team reviews its work when the cycle is completed. The accumulation of completed work through iterations comprises a release. When the project is deemed complete, there are project closure and post-project close activities which are necessary to bring any project to an orderly close.

Scrum – Basic Practices

Because agile project management derives most of its practices and vocabulary from Scrum and, in fact, is often (right or wrong, for better or worse) discussed interchangeably with Scrum, it is critical to understand the core practices of Scrum as the basis for the practical application of agile.

Scrum can be very simple. At its essence, Scrum uses three roles, three processes, and three artifacts as the framework for organizing and performing work. The three roles are the scrum master, the team, and the product owner. The processes are sprint planning, the daily stand-up meeting or daily scrum, and the sprint review, which includes a demo of what the team did along with a retrospective of their performance and how to improve (remember – PDCA). The three artifacts are the product or project backlog, the sprint backlog, and a visual tool such as a burndown chart, burn-up chart, or a scrum board, used by the team to see their progress during a sprint.

The team plans a sprint, commits to completing specific work, and then works for a specified period of time with total focus to complete that work. The scrum master leads the team in scrum practices and helps them self-organize. At the end of the sprint, the team shows the product owner what they've completed. The product owner reviews and accepts or rejects the work. The team discusses what went well, not so well, and what to keep doing or change during the next sprint. The team takes this right into their next sprint planning session, which ensures they can iteratively and continuously improve.

The Scrum life cycle (Figure 5-2) starts with the product vision – what problem are we solving and what value do we want to deliver to our customers? This drives the development of the initial product backlog – a list of features and functionality that the product owner considers necessary in order to deliver value to their customers.

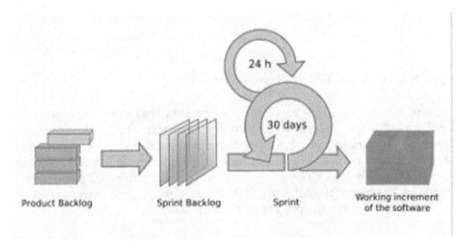

24 h

30 days

Product Backlog   Sprint Backlog   Sprint   Working increment of the software

Figure 5-2. Scrum life cycle

Release planning involves the selection of product backlog items that will be included in a particular release. Sprints will focus on a portion of that backlog for each sprint. Sprint planning focuses specifically on the work and tasks associated with each item on the sprint backlog, and the team finalizes their commitments while making specific estimates of what work will be accomplished in that sprint.

The sprint is where the magic happens. Each day, there's the scrum – the daily stand-up meeting during which the team discusses what they did, what they will do, and any obstacles preventing them from accomplishing those commitments. At the end of each sprint, there is a demonstration, where the team shows what it has completed to the product owner and other stakeholders. The product owner potentially accepts it all as complete or accepts some of the work as complete while rejecting other work items.

The team then performs its retrospective – it examines how it performed in the previous iteration, and what the team must do to improve its performance. During each ongoing sprint, the product owner and the scrum master "groom" the backlog – this refers to the ongoing process of refining and prioritization of items on the backlog to assure that the backlog items are progressively better and fully understood and that what is being done provides maximum business value. This process is repeated until the release or the overall project is complete.

Agile Practices

The next few sections of this chapter will take a practical look at various practices such as sprint planning, estimating, user story development, release planning, and other elements of agile project management. We will examine how they are used on their own as well as how they work and fit within a hybrid approach to project management where phase-based and agile practices are combined for the best outcome.

Backlog Grooming

Organizations and teams using agile frameworks and practices to perform projects should follow certain processes in preparation for each iteration or sprint (assuming they are using these defined time boxes – not all agile frameworks do). The product backlog, the list of prioritized features and work items, needs to be constantly reviewed and updated. Many call this process, particularly within Scrum, the grooming of the product backlog.

In practice backlog grooming requires constant attention. It can be hard for those new to agile to understand that this practice never stops – stakeholders and team members must invest some hours in backlog grooming every week to ensure that each iteration or feature planning meeting is worthwhile. As a practitioner I learned how important this is – first at Promega, where we got a good cadence for this going, and then at CloudCraze, where getting a consistent backlog grooming cadence in place was initially a struggle.

Product backlog grooming consists of three primary activities:

- **Prioritization** – Ensuring that highest-value items are at the top of the list, along with any mandatory dependency items

- **Discussion** – Ensuring that the product owner and the team develop and evolve a shared understanding of the work and features

- **Sizing** – Ongoing relative sizing of backlog items so that the team and the organization have an idea of how much work remains in the backlog, so as to inform other project and operational processes and decisions

As noted previously, this process must be constant and ongoing. If this breaks down or stops for any reason, the team runs the risk of attempting a sprint planning meeting without a groomed backlog of well-defined and understood stories. This in turn creates the likelihood that this work will be done in sprint planning, which diminishes its value, and also results in an inefficient sprint planning meeting. I encountered this problem in my early days with CloudCraze Software. A group of us came to a sprint planning meeting – I had created the expectation that the product owner would have reviewed the backlog and would propose a set of prioritized features for the nascent product development team to work on. The product owner had in fact not done that work, so we spent two hours doing it and then had to plan the sprint in a subsequent meeting. This resulted in the launch of the new sprint being delayed by a couple of days. These were days which, as a fast-moving software startup, we did not have the luxury to waste.

A constantly groomed backlog also means that the agile team always has a list of prioritized work that they can pull into an active sprint in case that sprint is going better than planned. Rather than stop and have to ask about it, the always-groomed backlog means the team can pull forward work and perhaps have a sprint that produces more output than originally planned.

Agile Estimating

Estimation of the product backlog enables a project team to roughly size how much work they are taking on or have left in a project or release. Estimation of the sprint backlog is critical to ensure that a team can make a realistic commitment for work to complete that is based on their capacity and their sizing and estimation of the work they are about to take on. Estimating in agile has proven to me to be one of the more challenging concepts to convey to people new to agile, especially if they come from a plan-driven project management background.

Estimating in agile projects requires a change in thinking. Agile estimating gets us talking about sizing the work, thinking about estimating in different ways, and using tools like analogous estimates to help us get a sense of what it's going to take in order to deliver the project, to deliver value through the execution of this project.

Let's consider how the plan-driven estimate might rely on processes and artifacts such as a work breakdown structure and decomposing the projects down to very fine level of detail both the deliverables and the tasks. Typically, plan-driven waterfall breaks a feature or deliverable down into a smallest logical component. Another thing that we typically do in plan-driven project estimation, and in fact is considered a best practice in plan-driven estimation, is that the person who will do the work, or somebody who is expert in the work, will give the estimate. We rely on a specialist or a discrete individual to do estimating of their particular deliverables and tasks.

Yet another assumption is that the entire project will be estimated upfront, along with a scope definition in order to lock this in. Then, we manage change very rigorously throughout the project life cycle. Again, the assumption is that the estimates are "one and done" upfront. There's the assumption that we're going to use estimates of effort and of the availability of resources to calculate the duration of any task and that we estimate and lock all of the features and functionality in at the start of a project.

Agile changes this estimating paradigm. For starters, estimates are happening at a higher level – they're usually being made using a "this seems larger or smaller than that" approach, and not going through the work breakdown structure effort to try to get to that level of granularity. We depart from the model of relying on a subject matter expert or the person who will do a particular task, and instead we look at estimating as a team exercise on the assumption that in many cases agile teams are going to self-assign work, so at the outset we don't know who may be doing that particular task. Therefore, the team needs to estimate so we have everyone's input.

Rather than locking estimates in at the start of a project, we update estimates regularly, and we assume there will be change based on learning. One of the inputs to this is performance or team throughput. As we move through the agile project life cycle, we are constantly assessing the team's capability and performance so that we have a sense of what can be accomplished within a particular timeframe, or conversely, what timeframe will be required to deliver all the functionality that the product owner may require.

Agile estimating focuses on a couple of critical things. It relies on the evolving items that are in the backlog or feature list. It assesses and analyzes the risk, effort, time, and complexity of those requirements to help get an understanding of what it will take to implement them and uses team capability as a way of measuring how long or how many iterations it will take to achieve this work.

Another change in thinking we have to make in agile estimating is a need to focus on outcomes as opposed to the specific activities that will be performed. Another way to put it is that in agile estimating, we are focusing on what we are going to deliver, as opposed to the effort that would be required to produce a particular deliverable.

This is where the concept of story points (which we are going to talk about next) enters the picture and helps us bring some analogous tools and sizing into the process. Eventually, we will factor in hours of effort, but this is not until we drill down into the task level and we are beginning to look at things on a more discrete level for a specific sprint. This doesn't happen at the start of the project, and the fact that estimation in hours is not done upfront frankly drives some practitioners and students crazy.

Sizing and Story Points

In order to estimate in agile, we need sizing and scoring systems. This speaks to a couple of different things. First, we need to define what we're going to estimate. Then, we need to develop some sort of scale to express our estimations. When we think about the basis for our estimating, we must also assume that we have a common vehicle to contain the work item or feature. Many agile frameworks or practices settle on the user story as the common method or language for capturing this. We'll look at user stories in more depth.

When we decide to use user stories, we introduce story points and other "unitless" scales as a way of estimating them. Some agile teams like to use "ideal days" – in other words, the number of days (assuming that the individual or team had nothing else to work on) it would take them to accomplish a particular piece of work. Injecting humor, but keeping in the theme of comparative sizing, there are teams that will use dog breeds as a way of sizing. They will say that a small story is a Teacup Poodle and a very large story is a Great Dane. Some teams may use measures such as a gummy bear or jellybean as in "that's a five-jellybean story." Again, the key here is that the team or the organization agrees to a unitless scale that the team can understand and everybody can use.

Story points are one of the most common methods of agile estimating. If we think of something being one story point, that's a very basic unit. When the story point is completed, you should have one relative unit of outcome. The complexity gets introduced as the team figures out the detail and scale. In other words, the team determines from the delivery perspective what is equal to a single story point, and they begin to establish the scale.

The team needs to think about the relative complexity and what it takes to deliver these increments. They may make up a scale of 1 to 10 or they may come up with a scale of 1 to 100. There is a theory of thinking that the orders of magnitude and the concept of relative sizing take us away from use of large scale. That tends to speak against the scale of 1 to 100 and points toward the 1 to 10 scale. You may be familiar with the Fibonacci sequence – 0, 1, 1, 2, 3, 5, 8, 13, 21, 34, …. The next number is found by adding up the two numbers before it. This is a common way of developing a story point scale. Many practitioners depart the Fibonacci sequence after 21, instead jumping to 25, 30, 50, and so on. At this point, the stories are too large to comfortably estimate using a relative sizing approach and should be considered placeholder estimates for these large stories, which are often called "epics."

In practice, teams used to plan-driven projects and estimating using a WBS – tasks – hours approach may struggle with or resist this approach. I worked with an agile coach (Andy) who shared with me a method he used to effectively trick some old-school software engineers who swore their work was too "special" to estimate using relative sizing into realizing this approach can be used on pretty much anything. Andy walked the developers through an exercise where they relative-sized the risk, complexity, effort, and duration of preparing various meals: a bowl of cereal, a sandwich, a dozen cookies, macaroni and cheese, a holiday meal.

I adopted and adapted this exercise to use in my agile project management classes and combined it with planning poker (covered next). Andy's developers (and my students) quickly realized that it was possible to size these endeavors relative to one another. It also served to show how additional refining questions (what kind of cookies? Chunky or creamy peanut butter? Does the definition of "done" include cleanup?) can help teams perform this relative sizing.

Estimating with Planning Poker

An exercise that can be used for relative sizing and estimating in agile project management is planning poker. This is a team process, and as we noted earlier, agile estimating is assumed as a best practice to be a team process. In planning poker, the team gathers, and everybody gets cards (that you hopefully have prepared in advance) that have the story points, the unit of measure assigned to them with the scales. You have a card for 1, 2, 3, 5, 7, and so on, or XS, S, M, L, XL, XXL, or whatever the scale is.

During backlog estimation or sprint planning, the team considers the story that is being evaluated, and when the signal is given, the team turns up their cards. What you hope to see is that the majority of the team has selected the same value, but there will be outliers – people who perhaps give a lower value or higher value.

The outliers explain their thinking: "Sean, why did you estimate that is being a 3 when most of us estimated as 5?" That's not to put Sean on the spot. Rather, it is to give Sean an opportunity to explain. He may have some familiarity with the work that the others don't have. The same may hold true for somebody who estimates higher than 5. That person is given an opportunity to explain their thinking. They may have unique knowledge that others on the team don't have. Having shared that information, the team will reset and then flip the cards again. You do this for each user story until you reach a consensus.

The reason we do this as a team is tied to the concept of cross-functional teams in agile. I give an example later of a handyman named Joe and his cross-functional team working on home-improvement projects. Because the person most expert in a particular thing may not always be the person working on it, it is useful to have the entire team's input on a particular item. For example, one person on the team may be an expert painter, but everyone else also knows how to paint to some degree. Therefore, having the entire team estimate how long it will take to paint a room factors in that the nonexpert painters may be the ones who, after finishing their other work, collaborate to paint one room while the expert painter completes a different room.

Iteration or Sprint Planning

If the team is using an agile framework that includes defined time boxes, typically called iterations or sprints, planning these sprints is a critical activity. Teams bring in a group of prioritized work that they can comfortably commit to and hold themselves accountable to deliver within that timeframe. The ideal outcome of each iteration of work is in increment of completed product that, standing on its own merits, provides value to the team and the organization.

Potentially Releasable Increments

Many agile frameworks talk about each sprint resulting in a "potentially releasable" increment of product. It is important to understand what that means and how that may manifest in different ways in different scenarios. A lot of people new to agile project management think they literally have to have a releasable piece of the product that could be customer-facing for every iteration – that's not the case. There are different ways of approaching this – a number of different definitions.

To provide examples: A skeletal design is a releasable increment of the product. A single complete feature – if we are thinking about designing a website, it could be that the completed logon page or the completed account setup – could be a releasable increment of the product. A key piece of the infrastructure can be a releasable increment. In the case of a board game that I designed and worked on with a team in scrum master training, the completed game board was a releasable increment of one of our iterations. We could not sell the game board by itself, but it was an important releasable part of the product.

If you're developing a technology solution, for example, developing the middle tier of infrastructure to support a website that needs to communicate with an enterprise resource planning system – in one iteration, we released the ability for a control on a web page to make a call from the control through the middle tier into the ERP database and return a piece of information. We considered that a releasable increment from that iteration. It may be something like the design and setup of a piece of foundation that's needed to proceed – this could be a releasable increment or vertical slice.

From the perspective of a magazine or book, you may complete the table of contents and say, "here's everything that's going to be in this issue of the magazine," or all of the chapters that are going to be in our book. It may be the selection of an issue's monthly theme and identification of everything needed to support it. It may be the story outlines for a particular chapter or for a particular issue. These are all things that would be considered thin vertical slices, releasable increments of the product, things that could be completed as results of an iteration, things to which you can assign a robust definition of done, and test and verify that they are indeed complete per the direction or the definition set by the product owner or the team.

None of these examples could stand on their own as a fully usable product. However, from the perspective of being complete in their discrete entirety and functioning or delivering value on their own, they are complete and potentially releasable (if not totally usable) on their own.

Note Be conscious of "fast waterfall." If a team considers the output of early sprints as a progressively elaborated plan prior to starting execution sprints, the team is really doing a "fast" or time-boxed version of plan-driven project management. This is not necessarily a bad thing in the context of agile hybrids, but something the team and the organization should be eyes-wide-open to.

Be aware of when a team is doing "fast waterfall." If a team considers the output of successive sprints as a progressively elaborated plan prior to execution sprints, the team is really doing a "fast" or time-boxed version of plan-driven project management versus using an agile framework and practices.

This is a perfectly acceptable hybrid approach to planning and execution – provided the team is eyes-wide-open to this and understands what they are doing. Given where the organization sits on the continuum, this may be fine in the context of the organization, the team, and their project - it is important that everyone understands what they are doing.

Sprint Planning Steps

Entering a sprint planning meeting assumes that we have everyone from the team inclusive of the product owner present, and that we have prioritized items taken from a fully groomed backlog. It is assumed that we start the meeting with that subset of items that we are considering for completion within the sprint we are about to launch.

The team reviews its capability – if it is performing together for the first time and it's an early iteration, they are essentially guessing at their capability and capacity – their velocity. If the team has performed together for a period of time, they'll have an understanding of the amount of work they can commit to within each iteration, and they can use this to estimate what they will be able to do. Based on this, the team reviews and commits to particular features or user stories that they will deliver during a particular iteration.

At this point, the team may do another round of relative sizing using planning poker or some other method that the team, as a self-managing team, has agreed to use. The team revisits only those stories or work items they are considering for the sprint. At this point, the team will break these stories or work items down into their component tasks. I often make a comparison to the work breakdown structure (WBS) in plan-driven project management. In agile, we end up with that work breakdown structure as a planning output, except that we are creating it one sprint at a time, assuming we are using a time-boxed approach in our agile framework and practices.

At this point, it is appropriate to estimate those tasks in hours of effort. This, along with the estimate of points compared with the team's average velocity and alongside of the available hours within the sprint timeframe acts as a sanity check to ensure that the team actually has the available time and capacity to commit to and complete the proposed work within that sprint.

Another critical process within iteration planning is writing tests or documenting done conditions. Whether we're talking about software, whether we're talking about product development, or whether we're talking about the development of a new magazine or website, on any project, there needs to be definition of, and agreement on, what represents done. This is critical, because at the end of each iteration, the goal of most agile approaches is delivery of completed components – things that can be considered done, and that on their own deliver some kind of value to the project and the organization.

Once the team has identified its work, completed its estimating, and agreed on definitions of done, it is time for the team to make a final commitment to completing this sprint backlog of work. At this point, it is important for the team to have some clear way of assuring everyone's commitment and agreement that the work is correctly defined and achievable.

From my friend and agile coach Andy, I learned the Fist of Five technique. In my current job as CIO at a community college, we have a technique we call the checkout. Both techniques involve showing one through five fingers or a thumbs up, sideways or down as a way of indicating full, partial, or no commitment to the plan for the sprint or solution to the problem. If a team is not fully committed, it is critical to resolve those elements prior to launching the sprint.

Demos

Another process common to most agile methodologies is a demo at the end of each iteration. Each iteration is to yield a completed piece of work – something that on its own provides some kind of value to the product owner or organization.

This is an opportunity for the product owner or other stakeholders within the organization to ask questions and to provide feedback on the deliverables. There is some indication from the PO of formal acceptance of the completed work or portions of the completed work at the end of the demo. This is also fed into the retrospective, which we will talk about shortly.

Performing this process at the end of each iteration allows the performing organization to establish the real measure of the progress that's taking place on the project and to see the incremental business value that it's receiving as an outcome of each iteration. Never skip demos – more on this later.

> **The best demo story ever**: Ecolab of St. Paul, MN, was an early adopter of CloudCraze as its ecommerce system. They had envisioned a phased implementation, and the first phase was to simply stand up the core product and start taking orders. This was to be an eight-week release with two-week sprints. After some initial planning work and team formation, we put our small team in with Ecolab's team for the first two-week sprint.
>
> As this two-week sprint came to a close, I worked with the client lead to orchestrate the first demo – it was going to be kind of a big deal, and everyone (including me) had a part in the demo. We were

advised that some senior Ecolab executives would be joining via web conference, and the client lead noted we should pay particular attention to any questions or comments from "Sam," a senior VP.

The demo went very well – every feature worked, everyone's part in the demo went well, and there were general good feelings all around. Sam, the senior VP, thanked everyone and then asked for the slides showing the product features. There was total silence for a moment – then, I realized that Sam thought he had been seeing "slideware."

I spoke up and said, "these aren't slides – you've been seeing working software and features delivered after a two-week sprint." After a brief pause, Sam said, "can we go live on Monday?" – followed by laughter, smiles, high fives, and so on. Clearly, the demo had gone very well, and this served as further motivation for the project team. In fact, it had gone so well that Ecolab approved adding another business unit to the ecommerce project before the original project was complete.

Retrospectives

Ongoing learning is a key process. Agile frameworks include the team's evaluation of its performance at the end of each iteration. This is critical so that the team understands what it's doing well and things that are not working so well. With this information, they can make necessary changes right away with their next iteration to ensure they consistently improve their performance – remember – plan-do-check-act.

Having an understanding of their performance informs ongoing and iterative planning. To put it another way, the project team has a better perspective or better picture as they complete each iteration. That in turn gives them an understanding of what the remainder of the project might look like so they can update the plan. They can provide an overall update to the product owner, stakeholders, or sponsors of exactly what the remainder of the project might look like. Again, there is the understanding that the overall release plan changes and needs to be fine-tuned with the completion of each iteration.

Release Planning

The release plan helps the project team and the performing organization understand what the overall release structure looks like – what they can count on. The release plan gives us an understanding of when we will be able to release something of value – whether it is to the marketplace, something available for purchase to generate revenue for the company, or something of value that is released internally to the company that gives value by providing the capability to the organization, or perhaps efficiencies that did not exist before.

A time-driven release plan shows how many iterations are possible within the prescribed timeframe based on the amount of estimated work to be done. A feature-driven release plan provides an initial idea of how many sprints will be necessary to complete the work determined necessary to deliver a minimum viable product.

At the core of release planning is the constant prioritization of features, functionality, and user stories so that the deliverables that will provide the highest value are at the top of the product backlog and reflected as such in the release plan. It is also critical that the project team and the product owner are working together and discussing mandatory dependencies as well as work items that are complementary. Overall release planning ensures that the product being built in this incremental way is coherent and that the order in which work is being done makes sense as well as ensuring highest business value items are completed as soon as possible.

Summary

In this chapter, we have discussed elements of agile and agile values that are important to know in order to help you understand how agile should function. Adaptive, flexible, iterative, and fast are all the elements of agile that are part of its values.

We discussed agile life cycles. We discussed how one version of the agile life cycle begins with what is essentially a period of waterfall initiating and planning work prior to starting sprints – a hybrid, AgileFall-type approach. We also looked at the basic Scrum life cycle and how it starts with a vision and backlog, followed by sprint planning and the sprint, and ends each sprint with the sprint review including a demo and retrospective.

In addition to providing foundational information about agile and scrum, we noted examples where practical hybrid application of these techniques would be the realistic approach.

Chapter 6 will discuss how agile teams should be formed and used and examine communication practices that often suggest these teams sit together. We'll look at whether that is always realistic and how to address this given the myriad of communication tools available to global virtual teams.

Agile Teams and Challenges

Special elements of Agile teams

Agile values "individuals and interactions over processes and tools" and "working software over comprehensive documentation" (Agile Manifesto, 2001). This being the case, it is important that any practical application of agile focuses on agile teams and their collaboration and commitment to working agile and functioning as a committed team. My own practical experience combined with countless practitioner and student discussions shows that building high-performing project teams is one of the hardest parts of project management, regardless of the approach. Adopting agile practices does not make this any easier – in fact, agile can make this initially more challenging.

Agile provides principles that encourage self-managed and co-located teams. Frameworks such as Scrum provide roles, events, and artifacts, but are intentionally not prescriptive in how to use these (that's what books and trainers do). One of the core tenets of agile is the self-organizing team. The team is ideally cross-functional, dedicated, committed, and accountable. Ideally, they are also co-located. All of these are easier said than done.

© Shawn Belling 2020
S. Belling, *Succeeding with Agile Hybrids*, https://doi.org/10.1007/978-1-4842-6461-4_6

> **Note** Agile traditionally valued co-located teams. As agile and the world evolve and confront change, virtual teams in agile are normal and very effective when supported with appropriate technology and leadership.

Challenge – Dedicated Teams

In my own career, I've delivered projects with and without dedicated project teams. It's unquestionably easier to deliver with a dedicated project team. Agile frameworks assume small, dedicated project teams, and agile projects face immediate impediments without dedicated project teams. Many organizations cannot grasp the importance of dedicated project teams for getting critical work done quickly and efficiently. Instead, these organizations spread out their people across multiple projects, creating the false sense that by touching many projects at once, they are somehow making progress on all of them simultaneously. This is a manifestation of the perpetuated myth that organizations must and can "do more with less."

"Do more with less" is senior management bullshit often heard in organizations that recently downsized or that experience rapid growth but can't or won't staff up to handle it. One area where this is especially prevalent is in delivery of projects, whether agile or plan-driven. Many organizations ask the same group of people to operate their business *and* deliver multiple projects to enhance the organization at the same time and then wonder why they experience poor results.

The "do more with less" approach creates scenarios where operational and production emergencies delay or stop value-adding projects. This approach causes inefficiencies while lowering morale and causing turnover and automatically puts an organization's projects at risk when the same people are doing everything. The risks come in two forms: tactical risks to the projects themselves and strategic risks from the delay in return on investment when these projects take much longer than expected.

Because agile focuses on rapid value realization, organizations that choose not to create dedicated project teams are immediately muting their outcomes. Practical agile values dedicated project teams and asks that organizations be practical in the following ways:

- They focus on delivering the vital few projects in shorter timeframes.
- They are willing to put the organization's best people on teams dedicated to these vital few high-value strategic projects.

- They prioritize ruthlessly to get these projects done quickly and efficiently without allowing production and operations matters to throw up unresolved impediments.

In practical agile, we do not delay high-value projects by assigning the people to handle production and operations and to multiple project teams. This applies to the business as well as technology teams. Every contemporary company is effectively a technology company – therefore, the organization's best business and technology people must be dedicated to value-creating technology-driven projects.

This is a significant change in strategic thinking and structure. Many companies organize and hire functionally and treat projects as exceptions to functional assignments. Agile requires companies to organize, plan, and hire based on value-creating projects and workstreams that can continuously transform the company. This approach also requires conscious development of organizational structure and hiring models that start new people and teams in operational and "keep the lights on" roles, while constantly grooming subject matter experts (SMEs) and technologists who can apply their growing experience almost exclusively to improving the business through value-oriented projects.

Identifying and correcting the risks and inefficiencies caused by the "do more with less" syndrome requires agile practitioners and senior leaders to examine resource assignments within their project and program portfolios. If the same resources are assigned to multiple projects and are also responsible for operations and solving production issues, the core agile tenet of dedicated project teams cannot be realized.

Regardless of the project framework used to deliver projects, the most successful and innovative companies *focus* their best business and technology people and organize around delivering critical projects. These companies outperform their competitors – not by doing more with less, but by focusing on a vital few high-value projects, getting them done, and moving on to the next while shielding these project teams from operational distractions.

If you ever need a simple and practical example of how this works, draw the following scenario on a whiteboard:

Imagine you wake up one morning and find that somehow, there are five massive boulders blocking your three-car garage. In the garage, you have two cars and a boat. One of the cars is needed immediately, while access to the boat would be desirable, and access to the other car can wait a bit longer. You have your significant other and two strong teenagers as resources, along with the assistance of your neighbors who have volunteered to help.

Would you

1. Spread everyone out across all five boulders and ask them to try to move each one a little bit throughout the day?

2. Get everyone together on the boulders blocking access to the first car, move that one, then the boulders blocking the boat, and finally the boulders blocking the other car?

The obvious answer is (2). Yet organizations choose (1) all the time by failing to create dedicated project teams and hold themselves accountable for disciplined prioritization and vigorous, focused execution of a vital few projects.

Challenge – Cross-Functional Teams

In addition to small, dedicated, self-managed project teams, agile also assumes these teams are cross-functional. Cross-functional teams are valued because, in theory, these self-managed teams can work more quickly and efficiently than teams made up solely of specialists, or worse, reliant on specialists from outside of the team. Does this mean that everyone on the team should be either a generalist or know how to do everything that the project work requires be done? No – this is not realistic and would introduce its own inefficiencies.

I tell my students and the organizations I lead or consult for to think of cross-functional teams like this: Everyone is really good at their thing, knows how to do one or two other things well enough to pitch in, and everyone is accountable for checking for quality and helping to clean things up. Here are some practical examples:

For several years, my wife and I were fortunate to know a handyman (Joe) who did a lot of repairs and renovations to our house. Over the years, Joe remodeled bedrooms, basement rooms, bathrooms, kitchens, and decks. Joe knew how to do several things really well, knew enough to take on some other things, and also knew his limitations. For larger projects like our basement office and kitchen, Joe assembled small cross-functional teams. Joe was a good project leader and brought in Don for detailed design and carpentry, and a couple of other guys for general carpentry. Don also knew plumbing quite well, and everyone knew how to drywall, lay flooring, and how to paint. When they needed electrical, they brought in that specialty for the specific task.

Both our basement office and our kitchen remodel projects had to be done in specific four-week windows, and Joe and Don effectively ran each week like a sprint, with a backlog of work to be done each week and goals for each day of work. When one of the team was done with his specialty work for the day, he would assist one of the others, and everyone checked out the quality of the work completed each day and helped to clean up the jobsite.

Mike Cohn, a well-known and respected agile writer and trainer, notes that cross-functional teams don't necessarily mean that everyone on the team can perform every task or has every skill. Cohn notes that "A cross-functional team has members with a variety of skills, but that does not mean each member has all of the skills." Cohn provides the example of having a highly talented database developer on a team. The intent would be to allow that person to focus on the database, but to ensure that the team had enough multiskilled members to complete their committed work within each sprint.

Cohn illustrates this with another example. A grocery store has cashiers who scan items and handle payment and will also have baggers bagging groceries. If the bagger gets behind, the cashier shifts and helps bag items. The multiskilled cashier/bagger allows the store to use fewer specialist baggers per shift (Cohn, n.d.).

Testing in software development is one area where cross-functional work has a significant impact. Everyone can test, or support the testing of completed features within a sprint to help their team meet their commitment. Some organizations like Salesforce have eliminated dedicated QA testers from their software teams and require all developers and architects on their teams to test. One senior vice president of engineering at Salesforce explained that everyone is accountable for quality and testing, and that developers rotate quality assurance/quality engineering roles during releases (Ayers, 2016).

Organizations must commit to developing the multiskilled team members desired for agile teams and projects. This is achieved through both intentional hiring practices and cultivation of cross-functional skill sets. Leaders and managers who want cross-functional people and teams will hire "T-shaped people." These are people who, in addition to having a specialty, also have other interests and skills that enable them to contribute to their teams in multiple ways.

Organizations must also commit to growing their own cross-functional people. In practice, this means that leaders intentionally develop project teams with the intent of ensuring cross-training can happen and also understand that short-term project results will be affected and accept this as desirable for the long-term goal.

Challenge – Co-location

Agile values immediate personal communications between team members and between teams and stakeholders. This is best illustrated by Alistair Cockburn and Steven Ambler describing how "warmth," effectiveness, and richness of communications are affected by the communications methods. In short, the most effective way people can communicate and collaborate is face to face, while the least is through hand-off of comprehensive documentation (Ambler, 2005; Cockburn, 2002).

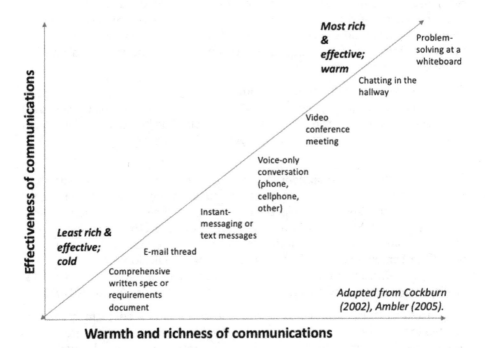

Figure 6-1. Effectiveness of communications – Adapted from Ambler (2005) and Cockburn (2002)

This speaks to agile's preference and premium on co-located project teams. The ability to turn and talk to a team member, walk over to their desk, or hop into a conference room or in front of a whiteboard is extremely valuable to the progress of the team and their work. As soon as phone calls, emails, and meetings are introduced into the communications stream, the speed and efficiency of the team is affected. Then, questions or needs for quick assistance instead become impediments, which leads to work not getting done in sprints and missed commitments.

Practically speaking, co-location is not always possible, practical, or even desirable. As of this writing, there is plenty of literature on the effectiveness of remote work and work-from-home options. I have led agile software implementation and development teams with team members spread across the United States and with customers in the United States, Europe, and the Asia-Pacific region, all with remote/distributed teams. Collaboration tools such as Slack, Teams, WebEx, Zoom, Jira, Azure DevOps, Rally, VersionOne, and countless others enable agile teams to create shared workspaces and collaborate in real time without being co-located.

Avoid the War Room Mentality

When it comes to successfully delivering projects, organizations should focus less on where team members sit and instead focus on how teams are organized. In my experience, physical proximity has less to do with getting to "done" than do the strong relationships present within a long-lived, cohesive team.

In one of my recent consulting gigs, I was asked to take over a troubled project that was over a year past its original scheduled completion date. When I was asked to step in, the organization's functional managers had already twice attempted to finish the project by putting the project team in a "war room" on the assumption that the issues would be partly solved by physical proximity.

In the case of this troubled project, the war room was perceived by the team as a punitive measure. Forced co-location is sometimes used with the dual purpose of ensuring that necessary people are present as well as providing an incentive to the team to get done and therefore be allowed out of the war room. When used as a punitive measure, it is not motivating for the team and can cause valuable team members to take their careers elsewhere.

Rather than jamming people who are not otherwise functioning as a team into a room and telling them to finish the project if they want to be allowed to go back to their usual working spaces, organizations must focus on creating long-lived teams that develop trust in each other along with a shared and deep knowledge of the products, projects, and systems they work on.

Such teams will be more likely to deliver no matter where they are sitting. Along with trust in each other comes increased and sustained knowledge of the products or business functions the team is working to improve. This in turn fosters increased productivity as well as increased quality. As well, these teams develop dependability in one another along with the psychological safety that enables highly functioning teams to creatively and productively debate ideas without fear of repercussions (Schneider, 2017).

Discouraging punitive co-location while highlighting the productivity of remote workers is by no means a knock on co-located teams. Physical proximity definitely helps teams rapidly communicate and collaborate. When possible, it's always ideal for teams to be long-lived and co-located. However, co-location of teams that are usually distributed or remote should never be forced or punitive. Whether co-located or distributed, successful teams are long-lived, cross-functional, and aligned with business processes. Organizations do well to keep these teams together for as long as possible, regardless of where each team member sits.

Practical Examples

During my time at CloudCraze Software (acquired by Salesforce in 2018), we brought our distributed software development teams together as we finished a release and completed our planning to launch a new release development cycle. These gatherings combined a celebration of work and socialization with release retrospectives and release planning sessions. Typically, the first day would be a welcome and introductory session describing what the program would be for the remainder of the week. That evening would be the main social event in which people who hadn't seen each other since the last release would reconnect and we would celebrate our most recent accomplishment as a team.

Day two would consist of a release retrospective inclusive of full walk-throughs of the new release for other parts of the organization like professional services, customer success, support, and other company executives. This provided an opportunity for the development team to showcase their complete release as well as provided the vital function of familiarizing the rest of the company with new features and any important defect resolutions that may have been completed. The remaining days were filled with refresher training on items like developing secure code or latest features from the Salesforce platform on which we built and then detailed planning to get ready and launch work on the next release.

Many other organizations using distributed/remote teams do something similar – periods of remote work are punctuated with team gatherings where the teams forge and renew personal relationships and work together for intense periods of time. For example, in *The Year Without Pants*, Scott Berkun describes the year he spent working at WordPress and how one of their practices was to gather their teams for working and social interactions periodically. Berkin describes how the combination of personal interaction for both social and work outcomes helped to strengthen the team dynamic and also get work done while the team was together and after they returned to their distributed norm (Berkin, 2013).

At Salesforce, a senior VP of engineering described to me how their distributed teams were in San Francisco, up and down the West Coast, in Florida, and some in small offshore groups. As with the other examples here, these teams would co-locate periodically when possible (Ayers, 2016).

Challenge – People

I sometimes get cheap laughs in my classes and presentations by saying "projects would be easy if we could deliver them without people." After the chuckles (and eye-rolling) stop, I typically speak to the need for respect and understanding on project teams. Working through the differences in people's work styles and personality types really is one of the biggest challenges in any project environment. The heightened commitment and accountability that are core to agile practices can exacerbate or highlight work style and personality differences, for better or worse.

The practical agile practitioner must recognize how this will manifest in agile environments and be prepared to use agile practices as well as other general soft skills to work through these situations. Agile's focus on the self-managed team and its collaborative efforts to deliver working product each sprint means that the most effective teams have to work through their people issues and develop the respect and trust that enables effective collaboration. Consider the following:

- Agile is totally collaborative and values real-time communication and people interaction.

- Stand-ups and retrospectives are critical opportunities for real-time feedback from other team members.

- To be valuable and useful, feedback requires both immediacy and respectful interaction that acknowledges and values differences in people's styles, thinking, and communications.

This means that agile practitioners must develop their soft skills and become proficient at giving and receiving constructive and respectful feedback, collaboration, and finding value in constructive conflict while maintaining respect for people and the team as a whole.

An example I like to use is the scenario where a newer team member has been sitting on an impediment all week. Look at it from the perspective of the team member, the scrum master, and some of the more experienced members of the team.

- The team member may be new or junior – they are somewhat intimidated by the experience of the other team members and fear looking incapable with the feature they are stuck on.

- The scrum master is wondering why this feature is taking so long but has to recognize how the new team member may be feeling while balancing the need and responsibility to help the team self-manage and work through impediments.

- The more experienced team members may have realized something was up earlier in the week and wondered why the newer team member did not ask for help.

- Everyone in this scenario must recognize that the commitment as a self-managed team requires the new team member to be honest about their impediment and for the rest of the team to be supportive and respectful while also teaching both technical and agile principles to resolve the impediment.

While assessing this situation, think about the experience, self-awareness, and professional maturity at play here. An experienced team and scrum master or agile coach may recognize and work through this situation with relative ease, while a new and less-experienced team and servant-leader could struggle with this. Recognizing situations like this one and others and even modeling and practicing them can help with the people issues present on all project teams.

Projects would be easy if they could be delivered without people.

—Shawn Belling, *bad punchline from agile course delivery*

Summary

In this chapter, we have examined some common issues involving agile teams. We've looked at dedicated teams, cross-functional teams, co-location, and virtual, avoiding certain mistakes like the war room, and reviewed some practical examples of how agile teams can be effective in co-located and virtual settings.

Chapter 7 will discuss the role of various agile servant-leader roles: the scrum master, the agile project manager, the agile coach, and others. Chapter 7 will also dive into the meaning of servant-leadership and its importance in agile and hybrid methodologies.

Agile Servant-Leaders

Leading vs. managing

Let's address this right away: The idea that a traditional project management background and the scrum master role or agile team leadership are incompatible or mutually exclusive is total bullshit. If you need any convincing of this, please know that one of the best agile coaches, trainers, and writers in the business, Lyssa Adkins, transitioned from traditional project management to renowned agile practitioner. With all due modesty, I've made the transition myself quite successfully. If you as a reader or practitioner are interested in these debates, jump online and enjoy. I'll focus on the role of the scrum master or agile project manager and the practical ways in which this servant-leader role functions to help agile teams self-organize and deliver value while constantly learning and improving.

In practice, many organizations have sought to convert their project managers into scrum masters or agile project managers. In hybrid approaches, this is an effective approach because these practitioners can apply elements from both waterfall and Agile frameworks as appropriate to the project and the organization.

© Shawn Belling 2020
S. Belling, *Succeeding with Agile Hybrids*, https://doi.org/10.1007/978-1-4842-6461-4_7

The success or failure of these efforts varies greatly depending on the organization, their culture, and their willingness to recognize the inherent challenges of adopting agile as an approach for getting work and projects done. The single most critical factor is the individual. Some people cannot make the transition from plan-driven project manager to the type of servant-leader that agile requires.

The key determiner is the personal and professional maturity and experience of the individual. If a person can carry around in their head different approaches to doing work while executing the work using these approaches, not only can they be effective scrum masters or agile project managers, they can also continue to effectively manage plan-driven projects. We're talking about work, not religion. As long as people can perform their roles effectively and embrace and practice the tenets of agile, former plan-driven project managers can be very effective as scrum masters and agile practitioners.

The practical reality is that many organizations have invested in project management as a business function. As these organizations make the transition to using more agile practices and recognize the advantages of organizational agility throughout the entire enterprise, leveraging this existing cohort, their skill set, and their existing knowledge of the organization just makes sense.

The mistake that some organizations make is thinking that one round of scrum master training or agile training and then certifying everyone will make for a successful implementation or transition to agile. Some of these organizations probably made the same mistake when they sent their project managers to PMP bootcamps with the expectation that the PMP training and certification would automatically make for effective project managers and successful projects. It doesn't work that way, regardless of the project management approach.

Having said that – scrum master or agile leadership training is necessary and valuable. This role is critically important, and training for this role will ensure that the aspiring agile servant-leader adds this to their foundation of learning.

The Scrum Master

In the Scrum framework, the scrum master enforces the values of Scrum and helps the team with the framework and process. The word "enforce" should be interpreted carefully. This is not a command-and-control role. The scrum master is there to remind, to coach, to help the team, to help them be organized, and to help the team get the most out of Scrum. The scrum master protects the team and acts as a process enabler. The scrum master, in short, does whatever he/she can to help the team accomplish their work and meet their commitments to the project and to each other and is always alert to opportunities to teach, learn, and help the team improve their practices and use of Scrum as a way of working.

The Agile Project Manager

The agile project manager role functions very much like a scrum master, but in practice is influenced heavily by how the organization is using agile frameworks and practices. If the organization is using an agile hybrid or an approach other than Scrum, the role will manifest in different ways. Anything that the agile project manager can do to help the team self-organize, stay focused, and do what they're best at is how the agile project manager provides value to the team and the organization. The agile PM will remove any impediments or obstacles that they are capable of moving and escalate any impediments that are outside of the team's control.

In many cases, the agile project manager retains traditional project management functions, such as tracking and reporting of project team progress into other business functions such as a PMO or other middle management layer. By performing these functions, they protect the team and prevent these from becoming a distraction to the team.

The agile project manager facilitates the various processes that are being used in whichever agile approach is used. For example, in Scrum, that agile project manager may be serving in the role of scrum master and therefore is facilitating Scrum process. They interface with the product owner or the project sponsor and in that role not only convey information and help the product owner or sponsor do their jobs, but they also shield and protect the team from the occasional distractions that a product owner or project sponsor or a stakeholder sometimes poses to the project team. The agile project manager also helps to shield and protect the team from outside interference from people who may have personal interests in the project, who may be coming from a management perspective without direct knowledge of how the team is functioning.

Servant-Leadership

Agile depends on a scrum master or agile project manager who understands and embodies the concept of servant-leadership. Servant-leadership is a deep topic, and I won't dive into it here. Start with the work of Robert Greenleaf if you are interested in deeper understanding of servant-leadership (Greenleaf. org). For practical agile, it's enough, but critical, to understand what servant-leadership looks like for the scrum master or agile project manager.

A servant-leader sees leadership as an opportunity to help others maximize their performance, enjoy their work, and achieve goals vs. seeing themselves as a manager or boss of other people who just wants to get the work done. As a servant-leader, a scrum master or agile project manager is not a task manager and doesn't ask teams to work harder or faster. Instead they focus on the team and seek ways to improve team performance, remove impediments, and provide resources that are needed to be successful. People who truly embody servant-leadership earn respect as leaders through their actions. Let's look at specific practical examples.

Practical Examples

A great way to convey what a scrum master or agile project manager really does is through practical examples. Let's look at how this role performs some critical functions:

- How to help teams self-organize during sprints.
- How to facilitate agile processes effectively.
- How to work with product owners to maximize their role and contributions to the team.
- How to use artifacts and metrics to benefit the team and communicate to customers.
- How to practice servant-leadership.

Helping Teams Self-Organize

Teams self-organize through the entire agile project life cycle. During initial project planning (whether done in sprint zero or waterfall initiating and planning phases), teams decide things like sprint length, place, and time of the daily stand-up, location, estimating processes, and other working norms. A scrum master or agile project manager can help the team with this self-organization and getting ready for their initial sprints.

The scrum master/agile project manager helps the team with these planning activities by referencing and recommending agile best practices and leveraging and sharing their own training and experience. They facilitate planning discussions and allow the team to take the lead while at the same time stepping in when necessary to steer the team toward best practices.

The scrum master/agile project manager could offer suggestions to the team on time and location for daily stand-ups, help the team reach consensus on this, and ensure a meeting space is reserved. Offering recommendations for the team be co-located in a single space and for the team to use a real-time collaboration software tool that is integrated into their office productivity suite in order to share comments, code snippets, and artifacts in real time are other examples.

A new team could be discussing sprint length and their estimating scale. The scrum master/agile project manager could remind the team that sprints should be four weeks maximum and recommend two weeks. If a team member advocates for a story estimating scale of 1 to 100, recommend using a modified Fibonacci scale, because training and experience points away from a 1 to 100 scale.

Scrum masters/agile project managers help teams make realistic commitments and facilitates this by organizing a meeting with the team and the product owner (PO) to review the product backlog, discuss priorities, and consider an initial set of user stories for the first sprint backlog.

Let's say the team wants to commit to 30 story points of work for their first two-week sprint. Because this is the team's first sprint, it could be helpful to recommend that the team reduce their commitment for the first sprint to 21 story points and remind the team that their initial velocity is a guess, and after a few sprints, their velocity will normalize. In future sprint planning sessions, the scrum master/agile project manager should ensure the team uses their velocity to make commitments. If the team shows signs of undercommitting, the scrum master/agile project manager should remind the team of rapid value delivery and ensure that commitments match their capability.

The scrum master/agile project manager plays an important role in the sprint review and retrospective by ensuring that the team gets feedback and recognition for their work and identifies opportunities to improve. The scrum master/agile project manager can organize a sprint review, which includes a demo of the team's work followed by the retrospective.

Some scrum masters/agile PMs use a survey tool to get anonymous feedback on the sprint they are completing and transfer that feedback to sticky notes. The scrum master/agile PM must be sure to note the team's velocity and committed versus completed user stories from the sprint to include in the retrospective. During the retrospective, the main objective is to help the team identify one or two things they could do in the next sprint that the team agrees will improve some aspect of their performance (once again – the plan-do-check-act cycle).

Facilitating Agile Processes

Scrum masters/agile PMs must be skilled at agile process facilitation, which can help to remove impediments like lack of access to the product owner (PO) or lack of a regularly groomed backlog that can slow teams if not addressed quickly. Without effective process facilitation, these impediments can impact an entire sprint and decrease the value the team can deliver. The scrum master/agile PM helps the team with sprint planning, ensuring that work is done and validated, helps the team run effective daily stand-up meetings, and helps the team handle the impediments that routinely surface during sprints.

Agile projects rely on consistent performance of certain activities to ensure that the team is able to focus on work that creates ongoing value for their organization. These activities include backlog grooming, user story evaluation and sizing, sprint planning, and sprint reviews. The scrum master/agile PM serves the teams by facilitating these processes.

For example, it is important to schedule regular backlog grooming meetings with the PO and the team to ensure a steady flow of ready stories for each sprint. It may be necessary to remind the PO and the team to balance customer value stories with mandatory dependencies and technical risks to ensure a coherent flow of completed work. It is also important to set up a regular occurrence of future sprint planning meetings at the start of every new sprint. Failure to do this can negatively impact ongoing sprint planning and slow the overall progress of the team.

The scrum master/agile PM facilitates processes like estimating, using planning poker or other facilitation process to help the team size user stories with their agreed-upon story point scale and facilitating discussions to reach consensus on sizing by ensuring that team members whose estimates differ from the team's initial consensus explain their thinking. The scrum master/agile PM also helps guide discussions to break stories down into component tasks as they start the sprint.

Finally, an effective scrum master/agile PM ensures that sprint reviews inclusive of a demo and retrospective are scheduled in advance to ensure availability of the PO, key stakeholders, and customers who should see each demo.

Rigorous Definition of Done and Avoiding Technical Debt

The definition of done is critical to the success of agile teams and projects. When teaching, I state that there is no such thing as "done except for…." I like to share the story of the first real scrum team and project I worked on. I was scrum master with four experienced developers, and we were really working closely to the Scrum framework and values. At the end of one sprint, in the morning stand-up prior to the afternoon demo, the team shared their updates inclusive of what they were calling "done" for the sprint and the demo.

One of the developers (Dave) shared his update and done items and described one as "… done except for…" and the rest of us nearly tackled him. We took this nearly completed story out of the demo because it was not really done. User stories must be totally clear on their definition of done, and it may fall to the scrum master/agile PM to enforce this rigorous definition of done.

This is how scrum masters/agile PMs help their teams avoid the accumulation of technical debt such as unfinished documentation or incomplete regression tests. By ensuring teams maintain the discipline of done and avoid technical debt, agile teams are always in the position to wrap up a release early. This means that if the PO is satisfied with the value delivered and is ready to deploy or release the latest version of the product earlier than the original release plan called for, the organization can maximize the value of the team earlier than expected.

Another important component facilitating the validation process: First, this is everyone's job – the whole team. Effective agile teams ensure everyone is accountable for the quality of the team's work and to help the team meet their commitments by sharing the responsibility of validation and testing. Note that the validation process must run continuously through the sprint. A common mistake is to allow work to accumulate to the end of the sprint and get backed up or, worse, be rushed through validation to complete the sprint goal.

The scrum master/agile PM should consider how to engage testers and reviewers early in the sprint as well as help the team break features and user stories down into smaller pieces that can be validated incrementally. Another way a scrum master/agile PM can help is to arrange for customers and stakeholders to agree to test or review work in progress during sprints and after normal hours to maximize the amount of work their teams can complete during their sprints.

Technical Debt

When I'm teaching, I use credit card debt as an example to illustrate technical debt. The concept is that you pay off all but $100 of your credit card each month and end the year not just with $1200 of debt, but accumulated interest as well. Technical debt is like that, too (Figure 7-1). It's not only the accumulated specific incomplete work that is undone, but also the additional effort and time necessary to work on what are likely various unconnected, noncomplementary work items left from sprints throughout the release. This adds "interest" to the accumulated technical debt and therefore additional effort and time to complete.

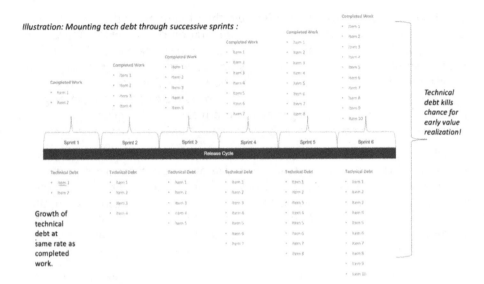

Figure 7-1. Mounting technical debt

Technical Debt and the Case for Demos

This is a good time to go deeper into technical debt, and how holding agile teams accountable to the discipline of doing demos after every iteration helps to avoid accumulation of technical debt and helps teams maintain their velocity.

Agile project teams that skip demos put their outcomes at risk – for each sprint as well as the overall release. The reason often given for not doing a demo at the end of a sprint is that whatever the team is delivering as "done" that sprint is not interesting enough to demo. After a couple of sprints where this thinking goes unchallenged, the team will not only accumulate technical debt, but their velocity will slow and progress on the overall backlog will slow.

Teams that demo every sprint tend toward better performance. Teams that skip demos tend to underperform. The reasons behind this deserve further examination to help build the case for doing demos every sprint.

The most obvious issue is that without the need to present a demo of what the team completed, it is easy to say, "we can finish that in the next sprint." Small things like documentation, bigger things like tasks, and processes like full regression testing can easily slip without the healthy pressure to be accountable for being "done" and able to demo at the end of a sprint. From this mindset, it's a slippery slope to accumulating technical debt and other partially finished backlog work that could require the team to add sprints to finish needed features, or to deliver less valuable scope in a schedule-driven project.

Teams That Demo Ship

Here are six solid reasons why agile teams should demo every sprint, even when they think their demo might not be very interesting to the product owner or other stakeholders:

1. **Commitment and accountability** – Agile project teams operate on shared commitment and accountability to themselves and to the organization to deliver on these commitments, every sprint and every release. Committing to complete a sprint backlog and then being accountable to demo what is done forces a team to be accountable to that commitment.

2. **Transparency** – One of the great things about agile is that showing what is fully done every sprint is a true and transparent way of measuring the overall project progress and leaving no doubt as to what is really complete.

3. **Healthy pressure** – Some pressure is healthy for teams. Knowing that they must demo their work at the end of each sprint adds enough of this pressure to help teams push themselves to get to "done."

4. **Pride in work** – Doing a demo every sprint encourages the team to be proud of their work every sprint no matter what they are delivering – even if they think the deliverable is uninteresting.

5. **Motivation** – Points 3 and 4 help with overall motivation. Project team motivation is an aspect of projects that is not always easy. Leveraging a degree of healthy pressure to deliver the demo as well as the team's pride in their work can go a long way.

6. **Agile discipline** – We demo because we are using an agile framework, and demos every sprint are part of the discipline of most agile methodologies. Rigor and discipline in execution is crucial to project success as well as improvement in use of agile methodologies.

Think the sprint deliverables aren't interesting enough to demo? Make them interesting! Find the value in each one and focus some element of demo or presentation around it. While at CloudCraze, I had an architect (Les) who worked for an entire release cycle on a set of application programming interfaces (APIs). These valuable, incremental software product enhancements did not lend themselves to demos, but that did not stop Les. For each sprint, he would pick a theme for his slides (*Game of Thrones, Star Wars, Family Guy,* etc.) and create a humorous and effective presentation on that sprint's API advancements with the theme. It communicated well to the demo audience and added humor to an otherwise dry topic.

Another story harkens back to my first true Scrum team (the same one with Dave, the "done except for" guy). Part of the team's first demo consisted of a blank web page with two fields and a control button. A numeric value was placed in one field, the button clicked, and the same value came back in the other field. Not too exciting – until the technical accomplishment of building first-of-its-kind middleware to communicate with a particular ERP system was explained. The product owner and sponsors immediately understood the value, making it a worthwhile demo.

In summary, demos are an integral part of agile projects. They are necessary to show the value completed each sprint and ensure the project maintains momentum. Remember: *Teams that don't demo will slip – teams that do demos will ship.*

Facilitating the Daily Stand-Up

I have been in organizations where the scrum master/agile PM's main role was to set up and "run" the daily stand-up. In fact, that was one of my main roles on my very first agile team doing Feature-Driven Development. I learned some good habits as well as developed and broke some bad habits during that experience.

My good habits included ensuring that less-vocal team members had the opportunity to provide input and advice and share their thoughts on team issues and technical problems. Another was taking quick notes so that on Friday the team could remember what we discussed on Monday. My main bad habit was not confirming with the team's functional manager her role and level of accountability – she insisted on being present but deferred any accountability for the team's performance.

Since the daily stand-up is the most critical meeting in agile (and in some instances, constitutes an organization's entire implementation of "agile"), it is critical to ensure this is an effective and meaningful meeting. First – know that this is not a "status meeting." The team is not reporting to the scrum master/ agile PM or anyone else present in the meeting that is not part of the core team. As Lyssa Adkins puts it, this is a commitment meeting (Adkins, 2011). The team is discussing how their work is going using the framework of "what I did, what I am doing, and my impediments, if any" to be accountable to the team and each other to complete their commitments in every sprint.

Scrum masters/agile PMs facilitate effective daily scrums by ensuring the team always has their stand-up space available and scheduled and reminding the occasional straggler to be on time and not let their team wait for them. My colleague (Dave, the "done except for" guy) tended to elaborate on how he did his work each day, and so I had to politely remind him to keep his update to the team focused on what work he did vs. how he did the work.

Our functional manager learned early in the project that the team met daily at the same place and time, and so she began to show up daily to listen in and occasionally interrupt the stand-up with questions. I found this to be pretty common behavior on agile teams on which I served as a scrum master or agile PM, so I learned to politely ask them to hold questions until after the stand-up and then coached them on how the stand-up was for the team to discuss its work and process and not a status meeting.

Identifying and Removing Impediments

Effective agile teams and projects are ones that can keep moving, and that means quickly identifying impediments. A key role of the scrum master/agile PM is to help and coach the team to identify impediments, to be open about potential impediments, and to raise them immediately.

Some common scrum team impediments include a need for a decision or input on a story to complete it, access to tools or resources outside of the team's control, assistance from other areas on work such as testing, and even simple things like supplies and snacks so a team can keep working.

An example I encountered while doing agile coaching and training in an organization was of a junior developer who did not share that they were stuck on a user story for fear of being judged by the rest of the team. This developer who had been added to the team partly to gain experience in working with more experienced developers was a bit in awe of some of them.

Part of the coaching and training I did was to remind the organization's teams that they share accountability for their commitments and must help each other succeed. That includes sharing impediments and helping each other resolve them as well as teaching and helping each other.

Agile teams are most effective when impediments that might keep them from accomplishing their daily goals and sprint goals are quickly identified and removed. The scrum master/agile PM must help remove them as quickly as possible. One common impediment is a need for a decision or input on a story to complete it. Therefore, the scrum master/agile PM must work closely with the product owner (PO) and when necessary track the PO down or get the information needed from other sources.

The scrum master/agile PM acts on behalf of the team to resolve other impediments. In one consulting engagement I worked on, the new agile teams wanted to use a software tool (Azure DevOps) that was administered by another area to track their sprints. The Azure DevOps admin was rather protective of the tool's configuration, and that impeded the team's ability to use it. In my role as an agile project manager, I convinced the admin to open the access needed for the teams and worked with him to ensure we could all use the tool effectively.

Scrum masters/agile PMs can add a lot of value to a team by doing little things like tracking down supplies (e.g., wireless mouse batteries from a street vendor in Lower Manhattan) and arranging for food when the team is staying late to complete work. Anything a scrum master/agile project manager can do to remove impediments helps the team focus on their work and reach their goals.

In summary, the scrum master/agile project manager is a servant-leader and agile process facilitator. They help the team self-organize and help keep things moving on behalf of and for the team. Scrum masters/agile PMs are responsible for facilitating ongoing agile processes like backlog grooming and sprint planning. They work with the team to define and enforce a rigorous definition of done and to ensure that validation and testing runs smoothly and consistently to deliver "done" every sprint. The scrum master/agile PM should ensure that the daily stand-up is an effective meeting and works to identify and remove impediments coming out of the stand-up and throughout the sprint cycle.

Working with Product Owners

The product owner (PO) role is a critical individual role in Scrum. A PO can make or break an agile team and project. To maximize the benefit of the PO role for their teams, scrum masters/agile PMs must collaborate closely with POs at all points in the agile life cycle. This can help avoid the impediments that can arise in the event of an ineffective PO and allow agile teams to deliver working product and value in every sprint.

Backlog grooming is the constant, iterative process of prioritizing, reviewing, and refining backlog items and transforming them into a steady stream of valuable work that the team can perform. In agile, a PO is accountable to ensure the priority of user stories and their value to the organization.

It is important at the start of a new project to discuss with the PO the backlog grooming process, its importance, and how to ensure that backlog grooming happens regularly through the sprint and release cycle. I've found it useful to meet twice a week to perform backlog grooming. Each meeting should include prioritization of stories, discussion of new and existing stories, refinement of stories tagged for upcoming sprints, and ensuring that those stories planned for the next sprint are fully defined and understood.

Release Planning, Sprint Planning, and Prioritization

Scrum masters/agile PMs and POs work together to ensure that the backlog items are groomed and organized into coherent releases and sprints. The objective of a team and the sprint is to produce a complete and working increment of product, every sprint. To do this, the scrum master/agile PM and PO must plan and coordinate the work and consider how all the pieces fit together.

Release planning is an important element of this process. The scrum master/ agile PM and, when necessary, key members of the team educate the PO on mandatory dependencies and technical risk items that should be combined with the high customer value items that a PO prioritizes. This ensures that the evolving release plan delivers customer value in each sprint. This also ensures the team delivers work that builds an ongoing foundation for the project as well as solving risks and uncertainties that could impede the project.

The scrum master/agile PM and the PO must consider the goal for each sprint within the larger context of the release and then work with the team to plan sprints that deliver the goal of incremental product value, completely done, in every sprint. They ensure that each sprint, while delivering value on its own, acts as a building block to the overall objective of the release of a new version of the organization's product.

Of the roles a scrum master can assume in an organization, one is coaching to ensure that all other roles are supporting the team and using scrum effectively. Since the PO role is so critical to the team's success and value realization, the scrum master coaches the PO as a key part of the job. The most common PO issue is lack of engagement or availability which renders the team and the sprint less effective. Scrum masters/agile PMs should discuss this with POs early, and, when necessary, often. It can be valuable to remind the PO of their importance to the team and to value realization for the organization.

Protecting Teams

Scrum masters/agile PMs are accountable for protecting their teams from distractions and interference during sprints and often must partner with their PO to do this. This is important to ensure that the teams stay focused during sprints and meet their commitments. Sometimes this means intercepting possible interruptions and having direct conversations with people who might distract the team.

Here's a practical example I have personally encountered: A sales executive interrupts the work of a developer during an in-flight sprint to discuss a customer-specific feature and requests the developer do the extra work to help close a deal or please a customer. At this point, the scrum master/agile

PM should intercede and reinforce that the team is in midsprint and that any changes to the sprint or release plan must be discussed with the PO.

Using Agile Metrics, Artifacts, and Reporting

Agile frameworks typically use velocity as a metric and tools like burndown charts and scrum boards to enable teams to self-manage and plan. The scrum master/agile PM helps make these artifacts and metrics valuable to agile teams and the organization and ensures that metrics and tools are visible to the team and owned by the team.

Organizations using agile need accurate reporting for overall project governance. A scrum master/agile PM who can synthesize this information while enabling the team to stay focused on their work is valuable to the team and organization. The scrum master/agile PM coaches and leads by guiding the team to maintain their metrics and artifacts for themselves. The scrum master/agile PM should use this same information as needed to maintain and provide reports required by the organization and its management processes.

The key metric in Scrum and other agile frameworks is team velocity. It is an important metric for determining the team's capability to commit to and complete work in upcoming sprints. It also helps in predicting and updating the overall time required to complete the project, or the amount of work that can be completed in a fixed timeframe.

The scrum master/agile PM helps the team track its velocity in each sprint and release. As a team works together for eight or more sprints, the velocity outliers – that is, sprints where the team had a very low or very high output as compared to their average – can be treated as anomalies when calculating velocity and planning future capacity.

It is also valuable to track the hours of effort that the teams invest in sprints. In practice, agile teams are sometimes pulled into nonsprint work. By tracking the hours that go into a sprint, you can compare these with velocity to evaluate the impact of nonsprint hours on teams' velocity. This data is valuable in discussions on having teams be dedicated to a single project.

Some teams assume that the scrum master/agile PM will own the scrum board, burndown and burnup chart, and related artifacts and metrics. However, keeping these artifacts current and useful is a responsibility of the entire team. As a team forms and organizes, it's important to discuss how the team will use a physical scrum board with user story cards and sticky notes for tasks or use their organization's agile management software to plan and track their sprints and the overall release. For example, a software development company may use a specific software tool to track metrics such as total story points, completed story points, predicted completion date, and unestimated issues (Figure 7-2).

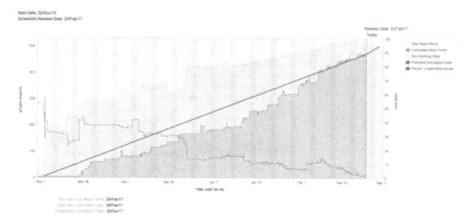

Figure 7-2. Example screenshot of visual release metrics in Jira

In practice, it is not unheard of to devote an entire stand-up meeting or to call a separate meeting to work with the team to update the scrum board. This is not a desirable outcome and should be reinforced as an opportunity to remind the team of the shared accountability for these artifacts. In these situations, it can be useful to remind the team that people outside of the team such as functional managers and POs rely on these artifacts to understand the progress of the project. I've found that these people are less likely to join and interrupt a daily stand-up to ask about progress when the burndown chart and scrum board are kept up to date.

Regardless of the project management methods, organizations need to know how their projects are performing within portfolios and programs. One of the roles of the agile project manager is to know the reporting and governance requirements of their organization and ensure that the artifacts and metrics the team uses can also feed the reporting and governance processes required by the organization.

While status reporting varies by organization, status reporting for agile teams and projects should include regular updates on velocity, updated burnup and burndown charts, and ongoing indication of release health. Release health is the likelihood after each sprint that high-level objectives or features planned for the release will be completed. This is done by showing features that are on track, at risk, or delayed (Figure 7-3).

Bi-weekly Update

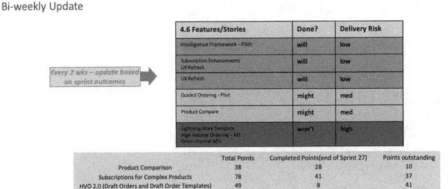

4.6 Features/Stories	Done?	Delivery Risk
Intelligence Framework - Pilot	will	low
Subscription Enhancements UX Refresh	will	low
UX Refresh	will	low
Guided Ordering - Pilot	might	med
Product Compare	might	med
Lightning Store Template High Volume Ordering – MT Omni-channel APIs	won't	high

	Total Points	Completed Points(end of Sprint 27)	Points outstanding
Product Comparison	38	28	10
Subscriptions for Complex Products	78	41	37
HVO 2.0 (Draft Orders and Draft Order Templates)	49	8	41
CyberSource	185	131	54

Figure 7-3. Example biweekly release health update

Practicing Servant-Leadership

Agile leaders must know the meaning of servant-leadership and embody these values every day. Effective scrum masters/agile PMs are servant-leaders who can guide their teams to focus on meeting their commitments in every sprint. Effective servant-leaders are invaluable to their teams, their organizations, and help ensure rapid value creation through the use of Agile.

Servant-leaders create an environment where the teams feel accountable for and valued for the work they do. A scrum master/agile PM should be available to help the team accomplish the objective, lead them, and guide them in the use of agile.

A practical example: Let's say a team is a bit behind on their committed sprint backlog items and will have to take action to meet their commitment. In a stand-up meeting, the scrum master/agile PM asks the team if they have ideas on how they could get back on track. The team suggests working late for a couple of days. The scrum master/agile PM encourages the team for reaching this decision, asks them what kind of food they want to have on those days, and also volunteers to line up people to do after-hours testing on the items the team will be working to complete.

Another practical example: Before the sprint review, a scrum master/agile PM should have made all arrangements such as booking the room, inviting the attendees, finalizing the presentation deck, setting up the conferencing system, and any other necessary arrangements. Then, the scrum master/agile PM should start the sprint review by thanking the team for their efforts (and any extra efforts as per the previous example) to complete their committed backlog items.

Servant-leaders help the teams they work with maximize their value delivery to their organizations. Simple things like taking care of the team's needs and handling the administrative work such as meeting scheduling and planning and creating reports and presentations allow the teams to focus on their work. More involved leadership work like coordinating with the PO and working with organizational project governance ensures that the teams have the information they need to make progress.

Over time, an effective servant-leader will help their teams make measurable and sustained improvements to their velocity and become models for good agile practices for other teams in the organization. While this type of servant-leader always ensures that the credit goes to the teams, the teams and other leaders in the organization will know and appreciate these skills as an effective agile servant-leader.

Summary

This chapter has focused on the role of the scrum master and agile project manager and their focus on servant-leadership in service of the team. Practical examples helped to illustrate how this role performs critical functions to help agile teams self-organize and maintain their commitments and efficiency in various agile project scenarios.

Chapter 8 will focus on the critical role of the product owner in agile and hybrid agile scenarios. The product owner (PO) is a role that can make or break an agile project and team, and understanding this role's importance and responsibilities is a key to success with agile hybrids and any kind of agile project.

The Product Owner in Agile

A role that can make or break projects and teams

My years at CloudCraze Software, my other personal experiences, and dozens of conversations with students and agile practitioners confirm that the product owner (PO) role can make or break an agile project or team. An effective PO keeps things moving and ensures that the team is focused on work of highest business value. An ineffective PO is a tremendous impediment and can single-handedly reduce a team's velocity to a crawl, damage morale, and mute the effectiveness of an agile implementation or project.

Note The most frequent issue with a product owner is that the team is impeded waiting for input or decisions from the product owner.

The product owner ensures agile project teams are focused on highest value outcomes during their sprints and release cycles. The product owner works with the team constantly to refine the backlog and answer questions as the team works to deliver on their commitments. The product owner also works

© Shawn Belling 2020
S. Belling, *Succeeding with Agile Hybrids*, https://doi.org/10.1007/978-1-4842-6461-4_8

with the team to consider the impact of user story and task dependencies as well as technical risk that impacts the delivery of work during sprints.

To perform well in this role, the product owner must fully understand the needs and wants of their customers. This role must also be available and accessible to the project team so that the agile team never waits for feedback or decisions. This role must deeply understand the key drivers of the business and emphasize these throughout the project to ensure consistent delivery of value. This role is so important that there is dedicated training and specific certification (e.g., Certified Scrum Product Owner) for the PO role.

In the words of one practitioner, the product owner can "make, break or impede" the agile team. If the product owner doesn't fulfill responsibilities to the team and the overall business, the negative impact shows up in a number of ways. Most frequently, the issue is that the team is held up waiting for product owner feedback or decisions. The fast pace of an agile team and project during 2- to 4-week sprints means that waiting for product owner input slows the team and reduces delivery of their commitments during that timeframe.

Another common consequence from a poorly performing product owner is a team focused on work items of lower priority or business value instead of deliverables of higher value to the company. This could happen because the product owner is not available or has not prioritized the backlog of work, and so the team spends their time on low-value work such as fixing noncritical defects. This could also happen if an unprepared product owner provides incorrect prioritization to a team because they are not clear on how the outcome will generate value.

These are just two examples. The product owner role is extremely important to successful agile project execution. As more organizations gain experience using agile, it becomes increasingly clear how impactful it is when this role is not performed well.

When identifying product owners, be sure that:

- **They are knowledgeable** – They must really understand the fundamentals of the business and the necessary outcomes as well as how they will provide value to customers.

- **They are committed** – They have a stake in the outcome and so will be fully committed, just like the team.

- **They are available** – They are not so distracted by other duties that they cannot properly perform the responsibilities of the product owner role.

Ensuring these three key criteria are met will help an organization select product owners who can contribute to high-performing teams and projects.

Product Owner Responsibilities

Successful performance in the product owner role starts with a clear understanding of the responsibilities of this critical role. An in-depth knowledge of the functions performed by a product owner can help drive agile projects to success and guide teams to maximize value delivery.

Project Inception

During project inception, the product owner plays a critical role in setting a common vision for the project. Some organizations prefer to create a document called a project inception deck. The product owner will lead creation of this critical document which captures the project vision, including what will be in scope, out of scope, and overall project expectations. The product owner then shares the inception deck with the project team, so they have the vision to refer to when planning their release work and ensuring it aligns with the vision as it plans its work during each sprint. By working with project stakeholders such as product managers at the inception of a project, product owners can create an inception deck that sets a common vision for the project that will be critical for maintaining focus throughout the entire project life cycle.

Backlog Grooming

The product owner is the owner of the product backlog and has primary responsibility for grooming the backlog. "Grooming the backlog" means prioritizing the items on the backlog, adding new items when necessary, removing items that are no longer of value, and constantly refining the definition of the items on the backlog. This ensures that the agile project team has a steady flow of valuable and prioritized items that they continuously work on from sprint to sprint and throughout the entire project life cycle.

The product owner adds new items to the backlog based on his or her knowledge of customer needs gained by being in constant contact and communication with product managers, customers, or other stakeholders. The PO removes features and backlog items which, based on these conversations, are no longer valuable. The PO reviews the project team's progress and, based on this progress as well as knowledge of customer priorities, regularly adjusts the order and priority of backlog items. This ensures that the team is working on items that are of the highest value to customers and the company as a whole.

Sprint Planning and Sprint Review

Product owners have several critical functions that they perform during sprints. They assist with sprint planning, ensuring that their knowledge of the overall product backlog gets the highest business value items added to the sprint backlog. Product owners are also expected to be consistently available to the agile team to provide guidance, answer questions, and ensure that the team is never impeded due to lack of direction or because they are waiting for an important question about a future or backlog items to be answered. By doing this, the PO ensures that customer-facing value features are completed and can be released so that the team delivers rapid and consistent value to the company.

During the sprint review, the product owner has several critical functions. The agile team has been working to complete sprint backlog items and has likely completed several features and components. At the sprint review demo, the product owner is responsible to decide if those items have been completed in a way that meets the definition of done and that deliver increments of product value or functionality as necessary to meet the needs of customers and stakeholders.

The PO should be present at all demos delivered by the agile team. In addition to seeing the work that the team has completed and having the opportunity to review, accept, or reject this work, the PO knows it is a critical opportunity to provide constructive feedback and encouragement to the agile team. The PO can also remind the team of the product vision and make the connection between each new feature and how customers will find value.

Value Realization

Agile is focused on achieving rapid value realization by delivering releasable deliverables on a regular cadence. The accumulated work of several sprints should result in a releasable product. It is up to the product owner to be thinking about and ultimately decide when the increments of product or project deliverables are ready to be released, thus providing their value to the organization and its customers.

An effective PO takes this responsibility very seriously not only during release and sprint planning but also periodically during the agile project life cycle by thinking about opportunities to deliver value to customers. The PO works with the agile team to ensure that sprint and release planning as well as completed sprints result in frequent release providing value to the organization and customers.

Product Owner Relationships

In agile environments, product owners work closely with customers, agile teams, stakeholders, and scrum masters. They must develop and maintain these key relationships to function effectively and fulfill their key responsibilities. They are required to constantly connect with these people to ensure that the project work meets the expectations and delivers value. Inability to collaborate with them can negatively impact the customer relationship, internal teams, and the organization.

A product owner must work closely, constantly, and consistently with stakeholders inside and outside of the organization as necessary to maintain a constant and intimate familiarity with their needs and interests. This is necessary so that the product owner can groom the backlog, prioritize, and provide guidance to the agile project team based on this always up-to-date knowledge.

Product owners must cultivate relationships with people within their organization who influence the projects they work on. In practice, this may mean meeting them regularly for coffee or lunch, attending their meetings, listening to their discussions and concerns. This also involves doing research themselves and maintaining a constant understanding of customers and the organization's needs and interests.

These stakeholders must feel a trust in product owners and know that they proactively work to maintain constant knowledge of their customers and their interests and know that they will use their knowledge and trust to prioritize work for completion throughout the release, during each sprint, and to provide constant guidance to the team as they work.

The Team, Sprint Planning, and Value Realization

Product owners use the customer and stakeholder knowledge that they accumulate to maintain another critical relationship with agile teams as they perform sprint planning. Product owners are responsible for creating a good working relationship based on mutual trust with scrum masters and the agile teams to develop and prioritize a sprint backlog and to negotiate with the team to finalize the goals and outcomes for each sprint.

Once these goals are established, product owners protect their teams from people who want to add additional work to the in-flight sprint and ensure that changing priorities are not allowed to impact the sprint commitment. They also ensure that the sprints are planned and completed in such a way that the release plan produces coherent, valuable, and releasable product increments on a regular basis.

One of the most important things product owners are responsible for is to help the agile team meet their sprint commitments by using their knowledge of the needs and interests of stakeholders and customers to provide guidance to the agile team during sprints. This relationship is critically important during the in-flight sprints so that the team never waits for information. Through this relationship, product owners share their knowledge and function as a daily resource to the team by answering its questions, providing in-the-moment feedback on deliverables to ensure it meets the intent of the user stories and creates the value expected by customers, stakeholders, and the organization.

Product Owner Relationship Issues

If a PO fails to maintain relationships with customers, stakeholders, and their teams, this will have significant negative impacts to the agile project and team. If product owners do not engage with stakeholders and stay current with developments, they cannot effectively apply this knowledge when grooming their backlogs. A poorly informed or uninformed PO offers no value to the team's planning work or offers incorrect information which could cause the team to work on features and stories of lesser value.

Product owners who fail to create strong relationships with their agile teams are not able to provide them with needed guidance or protect them from additional work during sprints. This in turn can delay or derail sprints and overall project outcomes due to this missing relationship.

Impacts of Product Owner Performance

A product owner's performance has a significant impact on the work of the agile team and its ability to deliver value, as well as the overall outcomes of the projects and products the organization wants to deliver. Effective product owners can add lift to their teams and organizations while ineffective POs become impediments to their teams and their organizations. Product owners should be experienced in their business and organization and receive specialized training in the responsibilities of product ownership in agile frameworks and environments.

Common Product Owner Failures

My personal experience, work with other practitioners, and discussions with my students show that there are four common product owner role failures that negatively impact agile teams and their projects:

1. Failure to lead on backlog grooming

2. Failure to maintain good and consistent customer and stakeholder relationships

3. Failure to be readily available to the team to provide critical information, direction, and feedback

4. Failure to be alert for and recognize when completed increments of product could result in readiness to release product or deploy new functionality to production

Effective and Ineffective Product Owner Behaviors

Effective product owners lead and own backlog grooming which means that the agile team has a steady flow of well-formed and prioritized items to bring into sprint planning resulting in on-time and effective sprints. On the other hand, product owners who do not perform this role effectively have a disorganized backlog. Their team does not have ready and well-formed stories for their sprint plans resulting in late sprints or poorly planned sprints.

Product owners who are readily available help their teams move forward without being impeded for lack of information. When product owners are absent or hard to reach, they create impediments for their teams, and the work of these teams suffers.

Product owners who maintain good relationships with customers and stakeholders have up-to-date knowledge needed to groom the backlog and provide in-sprint guidance. When this is not done, the backlog and the team suffer.

When the product owner is closely monitoring progress and completion of work in sprints and in aggregate during a release cycle, they can determine when it is appropriate to release a product or deploy to production. By contrast, a product owner who does not do this may miss opportunities to deliver value to the organization.

How Ineffective Product Owners Impact Agile Projects

When product owners do not groom the backlog properly, it means that the projects will not be focused on the highest business value items. It means that items in the backlog may not be very well defined, which in turn means that they may not be properly executed in the project. When a product owner is not engaged with customers and stakeholders, he/she cannot represent their interests properly which means that the project itself will not deliver outcomes that are aligned with the needs and interests of these customers and stakeholders.

When product owners are not available to the project team, the team is impeded in their work and the project itself can stall.

It is important to remember that a core tenet of agile project management is rapid and consistent value realization. The product owner's engagement is critical to make this happen, so when product owners are not engaged, they miss opportunities to release product or deploy new features and functionality to production, thus missing opportunities to deliver value to the organization rapidly and consistently.

Summary

The product owner role is a critical individual role in agile project management. Agile teams rely on this role to know the needs and interests of customers and stakeholders and to be able to translate these into backlog items. Further, agile teams rely on the product owner to groom the backlog, constantly refine the understanding of the backlog items, and extract the most valuable backlog items to bring into sprint planning.

Agile teams expect the product owner to be available to them during sprints and to help determine when backlog items are done and ready to deliver value to the organization and its customers. Effective performance of this role is critical to the success of agile teams and projects, but if the role is performed ineffectively, the negative impacts on the project and teams are many.

Familiarity with the responsibilities of a product owner, the key relationships that they should maintain, and the impacts of effective and ineffective behaviors can help aspiring product owners perform this role successfully and make important contributions to agile teams and projects in their organization.

In Chapter 9, we will discuss the agile coach. We will see how an agile coach helps organizations identify and act in opportunities to improve the performance of agile teams and team members. The agile coach can be particularly helpful to the scrum master, product owner, and senior leaders in agile and hybrid environments.

The Agile Coach

Helping organizations improve agile use and adoption

Organizations whose needs or interests in agile grow beyond one or two teams giving it a try, who are newly embracing agile transformation, or are attempting to scale their agile adoption will benefit from the role of the agile coach. Agile coaches bridge various roles in agile. They take a strategic and long-term view and will work across multiple agile teams and projects to help organizations using agile to get the most benefit from this work.

Agile coaches help the teams, scrum masters/agile project managers, product owners, and executives and other leaders in agile environments all understand and execute their roles. In addition to team and project success, agile coaches are also focused on enabling long-term change so that organizations can successfully implement their chosen agile framework and see tangible and sustainable benefits.

Agile coaches work with specific people and roles to help them better understand the role and identify opportunities to improve their performance in that role. Agile coaches will work with teams, observing their processes and communications in order to identify and share opportunities for team improvements. Agile coaches may provide just-in-time training, helping new teams leverage the basic agile or Scrum training they may have had by providing more applicable insight and situational examples to add dimension to this training.

© Shawn Belling 2020
S. Belling, *Succeeding with Agile Hybrids*, https://doi.org/10.1007/978-1-4842-6461-4_9

Organizations that are implementing agile at scale will create a cohort of agile coaches to assist their agile teams. Typically, these coaches will not only have significant experience and training in one or more agile frameworks, but they will also have experience and training with one or more of the approaches to scaling agile, such as Large-Scale Scrum (LeSS), Scaled Agile Framework (SAFe), or Scrum@Scale.

Agile coaching is something I personally have done a lot of, but not always intentionally. When I joined CloudCraze in early 2012, the nascent product development team knew enough about agile and Scrum to be dangerous and to aspire to using it effectively but had a mix of training and references. In addition to acting as a scrum master, I became the default agile coach for the whole organization. As I transitioned to leadership of our implementation delivery organization, I found myself coaching not only our teams but also customer teams in use of agile practices on our joint projects.

As a professor and trainer, I've provided coaching examples in classes and coached agile practitioners in exploring ways to handle challenges encountered in new and maturing agile organizations. As an executive leader, I've coached scrum masters, project managers, middle managers, and peers, helping them assess and address a variety of challenges and situations in various settings. Having done all of this, I have helped a lot, learned a lot, and above all, know that there are better and more experienced practitioners than me whose entire focus is agile coaching.

There are excellent books dedicated completely to agile coaching. The two that are on my bookshelf are *Agile Coaching* by Rachel Davies and Liz Sedley and *Coaching Agile Teams* by Lyssa Adkins. For truly in-depth and insightful reading beyond what my practical experience and examples can offer you here, I point you to these wonderful books by truly amazing agile coaches.

That said, I'll share here some practical experiences and tips that illustrate some coaching techniques and how coaching can be effective at various points in a project or in a team's development.

Coaching New Teams – Sink or Swim

Imagine being handed a new project and project team with no agile training or experience and being told "by the way, senior leadership knows that you are an experienced agile practitioner and trainer and wants you to lead the team and the project using agile practices." This is the situation I faced a couple of years ago while consulting for a large health insurance company that was figuring out that its usual ways of running projects were not always appropriate or successful.

I asked for a four-week "sprint zero" to develop a backlog and provide the team with some basic training in agile – they gave me two weeks, with about

2–3 hours total allocated to bare-bones familiarization with agile concepts and terminology. After pushing back and describing how the four-week planning and training timeframe would be a good investment, eventually I bent to my client's will.

The comparison I make to this situation is coaching a swim team that had little or no formal swimming training. The team plunged into their first swim meet and started a race without the benefit of formal swimming instruction. The team jumped into the deep end, began thrashing, and the only goal was to swim a lap and make it to the other side. Once there, the team caught its breath, assessed what it would take to swim another lap, and dove back in. In these early laps, style and technique mattered far less than striving to complete a segment and keep from sinking.

In a situation like this, as the team executes each sprint, experienced practitioners must be mindful of the need not only to coach to improve the team's immediate execution, but also to keep long-term maturity growth in mind. This means that the senior practitioners must be aligned on organizational goals for proficiency and maturity in agile frameworks as well as in overall project delivery. It is also important to be alert for team members with an interest and aptitude to take on scrum master and product owner roles.

Returning to the swimming metaphor – the coach must consider not only immediate improvement in basic technique to help the team complete the current lap, but also a vision of how the team could perform once they've mastered basic technique and are working on improvements in speed and efficiency. This translates back to our agile project and team as follows:

- **User stories** – Teaching a common format and consistently reinforcing the purpose of user stories

- **Definition of done** – Reinforcing a rigorous definition of done to ensure the team embraces value delivery each sprint and avoidance of technical debt

- **Improved estimating using relative sizing** – Encouraging the team to review and improve their assessment of user stories and their velocity to create more reliable estimates for every sprint

- **Commitment and accountability** – Creating and reinforcing the expectation that the team makes a realistic commitment for each sprint and then holds themselves and each other accountable for delivering

- **Efficient meetings** – Coaching so that the stand-ups, backlog grooming, and sprint planning meetings becoming progressively more efficient and effective

- **Impediments** – Coaching the team in quickly identifying and acting to remove or overcome impediments during a sprint

- **Candid and transparent metrics and retrospectives** – Facilitating and expecting transparency, accountability, and respectful feedback during sprint reviews so that the team is focused on continuous improvements in a safe yet demanding environment

Agile coaching with desired end states in mind through a logical maturity progression will help the team deliver continuous value as well as continuous improvement. Deliberate and intentional guidance from skilled agile coaches and team members will help the rookies progress through the thrashing stages and quickly learn to perform with both power and style.

A First Release and Sprint Planning Scenario

I was asked to coach an agile project team within an organization for whom I had done some agile training. They had an enthusiastic scrum master, a dedicated project team, and engaged product owners – a great foundation. They were attempting to plan their first release and early sprints and sought some coaching to help them.

I started by meeting with the scrum master to ensure she had the foundations of release planning in place:

- **The vision** – What needs to be built, and how it will provide value to customers and the organization.

- **A product owner** – Someone with the knowledge and passion to own the vision and to provide information and direction to ensure the team builds with that vision and value in mind.

- **A team** – A dedicated cross-functional team to deliver this project.

- **A backlog** – Work with the product owner to create a wish list of the capabilities needed to provide the desired value.

- **Refine the backlog into user stories** – The team and subject matter experts used their training to turn the wish list into user stories.

- **Prioritization** – The team worked with the product owner to prioritize the backlog and user stories.

- **Decision on sprint length** – The team determines the length of their sprints: no longer than four weeks.

- **Rough idea of how many sprints** – The team and the organization develop a rough idea (subject to ongoing refinement) of how many sprints might be necessary, or that they are willing to invest in the release, to achieve the desired outcome and value.

Coming on the heels of a multiday investment in agile training, this seemed like a lot of work to the functional managers who had not participated, but it was a critical investment necessary to ensure the first release to be delivered using agile provided value to their organization. This first sprint set the team up for success, and the first release would set the tone for successful agile transformation and use of agile on future projects.

Once the foundational work was complete, I returned and met with the whole team inclusive of product owners and functional managers. We worked through seven steps to create their first release plan.

Step 1 – Prioritize the backlog of user stories using the MoSCoW rules (Must Have, Should Have, Could Have, Wish/Won't Have).

Step 2 – Use t-shirt sizing to size the user stories; keep it simple: use XS–XL.

Step 3 – Organize the user stories into sprints based on the team's gut feel and initial understanding of the project.

Step 4 – Overlay a numeric scale to the t-shirt scale (1, 2, 3, 5, 7, 9, 11, 15, 21, or similar), and then update the user story sizing, replacing the t-shirt scale with the numeric scale.

Step 5 – Estimate initial velocity. How many points of work does the team think they can complete in their first sprint? This is a total guess for new teams and will fluctuate in the early sprints.

Step 6 – For Sprint 1, identify the tasks required for each user story and estimate these in hours.

Step 7 – Develop a solid plan for Sprint 1, a soft plan for Sprint 2: it will be revised based on the team's experience in their first sprint.

Completing these seven steps in collaboration with an experienced agile coach (in this case, me) enabled the team to exit their first release and sprint planning session with an initial release plan as well as a solid plan for their first sprint. This in turn positioned that team for a successful opening sprint, which delivered value to the organization and earned credibility for the team and the initial use of agile practices.

Coaching During Sprints

Coaching teams in their daily stand-ups and their normal work routines is like coaching a sports team during an event. The opportunities to coach come at breaks in the action and coaching must be offered without disrupting the flow of the game. In some instances, the coach may have the opportunity to take a player aside and offer tips prior to sending them back into the game. In rare instances, the coach may call a time-out to address a specific issue or reset the team if they've gotten away from the game plan.

New teams may benefit from reminders that agile thrives on team collaboration and commitment. One issue I have encountered is the tendency of teams and individuals to focus on individual assignments rather than treat the work as commonly owned by the entire team. In agile, "my tasks versus your tasks" is the wrong way to think. Teams used to getting task assignments and then focusing on "their" work will, without successful coaching to get past this, not adopt agile ways of working.

It is worth noting now that the behavior described here is less likely to occur if the organization itself has moved away from individual reward (i.e., individual bonuses and other performance-based variable compensation) and moved toward team-focused incentives. Because agile works best with team accountability and commitment, it follows that any incentives reward the team to think about "our work" versus "my work."

Coaching in Sprint Reviews

Sprint reviews are excellent opportunities to observe and to coach agile teams. The coach sees the work product from the sprint, hears feedback from the product owner and other stakeholders, and sees and hears the team's own assessment of how things went. Much like a coach evaluating a team's performance after a game and working with key team members to identify specific items to focus on for the next game, the agile coach works with the scrum master/agile PM and product owner to identify specific things to improve on for the next sprint. Remember —plan-do-check-act.

Sprint reviews are also good opportunities to help a scrum master/agile PM address some common issues with daily stand-ups. Agile coaches can help with issues like:

- The team member whose update to the team every stand-up is "worked on bugs, working on bugs, no impediments."

- The update given by a team member for the last three stand-ups indicates that they are impeded somehow, but they have not indicated this or asked for help.

- The team provides standard updates but is not problem-solving or collaborating on impediments or making sprint commitments.

Coaching at Releases

If coaching at sprint reviews is like coaching after each game, then releases are like coaching a team at the end of a season. The release retrospective and release planning provide opportunities to help a team evaluate their performance over an extended period of time. Review of the sprint retrospectives and any incremental improvements the team made throughout the release cycle will help to build a picture of the team's learnings, progress, and improvement. This will also reveal items the team may have identified but either failed to address or were beyond the team's power to address.

In the breaks between releases, the agile coach can also identify, recommend, and help deliver specific training that could help the team and the organization as a whole improve and grow its adoption and implementation of agile. We did this at CloudCraze – in 2016, I added an experienced agile coach and scrum master to the development organization. In our subsequent onsite gatherings as we wrapped one release and started up the next, we assessed the outcomes from the sprint retrospectives during the release as well as our assessment of the overall process improvements needed and geared specific training sessions to these needs.

Summary

These examples have shown you how an agile coach can work in different scenarios with a team to help them become more effective. The agile coach helps teams and organizations improve their use of agile and the value that they get from the practices and the projects they deliver by doing so.

The next chapter begins Part 3 of the book: advanced topics in agile. Chapter 10 discusses design thinking. Design thinking is an approach to product development that helps the practitioner really understand the customer and what problem they're trying to solve. Design thinking takes that understanding of the customers' perspective and uses rapid prototyping to gain feedback before reaching a decision on what product to develop. Design thinking with agile helps the project team and the organization work closely with customers and rapidly determine the best product to build using agile.

Advanced Topics in Agile

Design Thinking with Agile

Shared concepts and applications

I had an aversion to the phrase "fail fast" for many years. To me, it implied a sense of carelessness and was a reminder of the first .com boom and bust, in which plenty of early .com companies did indeed fail fast because they did not value nor pay any attention to basic business fundamentals. As I learned more about agile and design thinking, the idea of "fail fast" morphed (for me) into an understanding that this meant building working prototypes to get early customer feedback as well as attempting technically challenging work early, all for the purpose of learning from early "failures."

I still don't think it is accurate to call these early prototypes "failures." Practically speaking, these are really not failures but rather iterative prototypes that help turn early information on the needs and wants of the customer into working models that customers can interact with. This iterative process is (to me) more like a series of successes than failing fast – but I did not create design thinking or its vocabulary, so we're stuck with "fail fast." In addition to discussing how agile and design thinking are complementary approaches to creating and delivering solutions, I'll share two practical examples showing how the hybrid of design thinking and agile helped teams and organizations I led deliver some innovative, customer-focused technology products.

© Shawn Belling 2020
S. Belling, *Succeeding with Agile Hybrids*, https://doi.org/10.1007/978-1-4842-6461-4_10

As we get started, please note that in addition to my own experiences described here, I reviewed some excellent source materials including a *Harvard Business Review* article and a TED Talk by Tim Brown (2008), a TEDx Berkeley talk by Guy Kawasaki (The Art of Innovation, 2014), videos and articles from the Neilsen Norman Group, and a YouTube video by William Burnett of Stanford on design thinking (2016). These sources provided historical materials for the origins of design thinking and solidified my understanding of design thinking and its relationship to agile practices.

What Is Design Thinking?

Design thinking is a user-centric method for developing solutions that meet customer needs. When used in combination with agile practices, design thinking can help organizations identify customer needs and rapidly iterate through prototypes that ultimately enable organizations to design and create solutions that provide value to their customers. Design thinking and agile both leverage foundational concepts and mindsets that are, in some cases, new, different, and potentially challenging for organizations to implement.

Design thinking is usually attributed to Roger Martin of the Rotman School; David Kelley, founder of IDEO; and Tim Brown, CEO of IDEO – all three are influential in naming the process of design thinking and the evolution and advancement of design thinking, starting in the 1990s. The approaches that are used in design thinking trace back even farther (much like the methods that form the roots of agile and Scrum), but like agile and Scrum, became well-known more recently (1990s) through the work of these and other prominent thinkers and practitioners (Gibbons, 2016).

Design thinking takes practitioners through specific phases culminating in a testable prototype that, if successful with customers, is ready for the organization to implement. Agile practices are supported by design thinking and also support aspects such as rapid prototyping and implementation. There are similarities between design thinking and agile practices which allow organizations already using agile methods to incorporate design thinking processes without major changes to their existing processes.

Shared Concepts – Agile and Design Thinking

Design thinking shares several elements with agile practices. The customer-centric approach and the use of rapid and iterative prototypes with the expectation that customer feedback will steer the team toward the best outcome are shared by design thinking and agile. Both practices are centered around the human experience and require that we understand the customer context in order to fully comprehend the problem or opportunity for which we want to design a new product or service offering.

Both agile and design thinking require input from outside of the teams working on the product. Most frequently, this comes through close interaction with customers. For design thinking, this may be user research, business needs, and technology possibilities. For software development, this may be backlogs, user stories, and success metrics (Cooper-Wright, 2016). Both agile and design thinking leverage iterative and ongoing refinement. Empathy and empowerment are key shared concepts that both enable teams to empathize with customers as well as the empowerment to bring that experience into their work.

User-Focused Design

Design thinking and agile leverage user-focused design. The agile concept of the "user story" with its focus on value outcomes for the customer or user supports this concept. The concept is shared with design thinking in that design thinking asks that the teams place themselves in the customer's "world" and form some theories about what the customers might want based on this empathy. In two examples I'll share later, we'll see how viewing the world through the lived experiences of your customer helps with the design and development of products and solutions.

Problem-Solving

Problem-solving with design thinking and agile is different from many other processes. I think the biggest difference is that both techniques begin without assuming research and data will be collected upfront. Other approaches to product and software development assume that a lot of quantitative data and detailed requirements will be gathered before starting. However, agile project methods and design thinking methods assume that qualitative data will be gathered through empathetic experiences with customers at the start of the process.

Cross-Functional Teams

Agile and design thinking rely on multidisciplinary cross-functional teams in order to achieve success. Rather than reach outside of the team to get specific information or expertise when needed, both approaches assume that various disciplines such as creative, engineering or technical, user experience, testing, content – whatever it takes – will be part of a cohesive team. This is easier said than done, as it is likely that some challenges will arise in this environment.

It is critical that all the disciplines respect each other's specialties and recognize that pitching in outside of one's specialty is critical to creating great outcomes.

Rapid Prototyping with Customer Feedback

Agile and design thinking are rooted in the concept of getting working prototypes in front of customers and then responding to their feedback. In agile, this is baked into the sprint review and demo at the end of each of an agile team's sprint. In design thinking, the concept is applied to build rapid and inexpensive prototypes. These could be wireframes for software user interfaces, click-through demo pages, or inexpensive working models of products. However they manifest, these rapid prototypes allow customers to interact with the prototype and provide feedback at a point in the process where changes can be made quickly and cheaply. As customers interact with the prototypes, they can offer ideas that can be immediately incorporated into the next prototype and tested or experienced to see how they really work and feel to customers.

Failing Fast Revisited

Earlier, I complained about the phrase "failing fast." As I noted, before I really understood what it meant in the context of agile and then design thinking, it sounded to me like "working carelessly." Clearly not the case.

In agile and design thinking, failing fast means using rapid prototyping to find out quickly what works and what does not work – whether from the customer's perspective or from a technical achievement perspective. The early prototypes that fail to meet customer's needs still provide valuable information through the customer's responses and reactions to them. The same applies to technical experiments that show the team what does not work while iterating toward what does.

This in turn helps each successive prototype get closer and closer to something that will really work. In this way, the fast pace of rapid prototyping and the learning from each "failure" allow the teams to essentially fail quickly and iteratively toward a successful outcome that will meet the customer's needs as well as enable the development and construction of a successful product.

Alignment – Agile and Design Thinking

The phases and processes of design thinking don't necessarily align exactly with agile processes. They do, however, strongly support agile projects and help to provide foundational elements that both support and align with the way agile projects are run. Design thinking uses a process in which the phases help the agile team create new and innovative solutions to meet customer needs and help solve a specific problem. They help the agile team lay a solid foundation for a successful project that will deliver value by meeting customer's needs through innovative products and solutions.

Design Thinking Phases

Design thinking typically uses these phases: empathize, define, ideate, prototype, and test. Some organizations will add implement to these phases. Agile projects can align with these phases depending on where the agile project is in its life cycle. Assuming the phases and the agile project are both at inception, the design thinking phases can work in concert to provide the agile project inputs and outputs needed to move the project forward.

As design thinking's empathize and define phases lead to definition of a problem statement, this aligns with the agile practice of creating a vision statement which in turn is an important part of the inception process of an agile project. The ideation phase in design thinking can lead to user stories, and the rapid prototyping lends itself to time-boxed agile sprints that end with demos and get prototypes into the hands of customers to test.

Design Thinking Activities

The empathize phase activities are not purely about understanding the discrete needs of the customer but also about fully understanding the environment in which the customer exists and how that shapes their needs. By directly observing the customer and their environment, design thinking and agile can derive data that creates not only empathy but starts the process of feature and user story development that helps to create the agile project's product backlog.

Some organizations (like the two examples we'll review shortly) go into the field with their customers to gain experience. Ideation can extend this work further as the team considers ideas that could address the problems they've discovered through this field empathy work. An organization's activities at this point may not be specifically called "ideation," but likely will follow their field activities as teams discuss what they have seen and learned and begin to develop ideas of how they could address the needs and problems they have witnessed and are beginning to understand.

Design thinking phases are intended to be performed sequentially. This sequence aligns in some ways to the agile life cycle and helps lay a foundation for a successful agile project. The empathize phase in which direct observation and collection of quantitative data is performed ensures that the project team fully understands the customer's context as well as their needs prior to the creation of user stories. The define phase ensures that the customer problem or need is defined clearly and enables the agile team to create a vision statement for the project that resonates with the entire team. Ideation provides the agile team the opportunity to consider a variety of possible solutions prior to rapid prototyping.

Outcomes

Application of design thinking within the context of agile projects provides key outcomes that, as noted earlier, create solid foundational elements that can help to enable a successful project outcome. Empathizing with customers helps the agile team really understand their needs and ensures that they keep the customer's context and lived experiences in mind when they are designing solutions and creating and testing them.

Clearly defining the problem is an important outcome and input to the agile project in that it enables the creation of the vision statement that is part of project inception. Ideation leads to options to solve the problem and deliver the vision that can then be rapidly prototyped. Ideas not only help to define possible prototypes, but also enable the creation of the user stories that the agile team needs to attempt to develop these prototypes. Testing validates the solutions with customers as well as ultimately defines whether the agile team has delivered something of value to customers through their work in each sprint.

Practical Examples – Design Thinking with Agile

From 2005 to 2012, I worked for a biotechnology firm in Madison, Wisconsin, called Promega Corporation. This is where I first worked using a hybrid of agile and design thinking practices, both intentionally and unintentionally. In 2012, I joined a consulting firm that included an ecommerce software startup called CloudCraze, which in 2018 became part of Salesforce. While with CloudCraze, I continued to learn more about and use agile and design thinking to develop and implement our ecommerce software product. The following are two practical examples that illustrate the use of a hybrid of agile and design thinking to develop and deliver software products.

Promega and STR Normalization Manager

Have you ever watched one of those CSI shows where the crime scene investigators drop a DNA sample off at the crime lab and hours later get to see a 3-D touchscreen showing who the suspect is and where they are located? DNA analysis doesn't work like that. Crime labs around the country are backed up with unprocessed DNA samples because it is a precise and painstaking process that can be accelerated to some extent with laboratory automation and robotics and software.

Promega sought to improve part of this process through the normalization of DNA samples. Depending on the quality of a DNA sample, it yields a "signal" that varies in strength. When using laboratory automation, normalizing this signal is critical to accurate and consistent results. Promega R&D scientists and bioinformatics researchers conceived a prototype DNA normalization software tool and wanted to bring it to market. That's where my colleagues and I got involved. The CEO asked our IT leader to provide a team to collaborate with product management and R&D to harden the prototype and develop it as commercial-grade software.

Promega's customers were crime lab scientists. Promega had former CSIs and crime lab managers on the product management team for this project. This enabled our team to use user-centric design to develop lab automation software to help these scientists process DNA samples more efficiently. Their ideas on what these customers might want in a future product combine with the user story and backlog process. Rather than try surveys and focus groups, the scientists worked directly from their customer's point of view. Promega's own human identity scientists also provided a customer-centric input, as they both used and tested the initial prototype and subsequent iterative prototypes.

Our team consisted of two former crime lab managers as product managers, two scientists, an informatics developer, a UX designer, two software developers, and a project manager. This multidisciplinary cross-functional team collaborated to empathize with and define their customers' problems and then ideate solutions. Using the rapid prototyping approach, we created prototypes of the software that would normalize the signals from various DNA samples and create a file optimized for specific laboratory automation equipment. The team demo'd to crime lab customers as well as internal scientists for feedback. The feedback from both external and internal customers enabled the team to rapid prototype through versions with enhanced internal testing features and user interface improvements.

We quickly moved into a cadence of rapid prototyping that put a new version of the software in front of our internal and external customers every week. Internal customers would test immediately and provide feedback on new or revised features, while the product managers – the former crime lab people – would get versions to their customers and solicit feedback that could be incorporated into the product. Halfway into the scheduled project timeline, the prototype was solid enough to install in a crime lab for a prominent national law enforcement agency for a week of onsite testing. We ultimately completed and shipped the 1.0 version of the software in time for a major industry tradeshow.

CloudCraze and Coca-Cola

Some of the early adopters of CloudCraze's B2B ecommerce system were Coca-Cola bottling groups in the United States, Germany, and Belgium, the first being the group that bottled and sold Coca-Cola products in Belgium and the Netherlands. In order to better understand how the owners of small stores and distributors in these markets placed orders with this Coca-Cola bottler to in turn understand how to design an ecommerce system that would work for them, a team from Coca-Cola and CloudCraze spent days in the field observing how these customers worked and what problems they faced when ordering and reordering product.

Our CloudCraze development team consisted of a product manager with deep experience on both sides of B2B, a software architect experienced in front-end and back-end development, another developer with more front-end and UX experience, and a project manager. We learned from Coca-Cola's customers that they needed to be able to start a product inventory refill order on their tablets or smartphones while walking the shelves in the warehouse or store, and then continue the order on their desktop computer. Leveraging this user-centric perspective along with agile practices, we defined the problem and thought about how we could adapt our software and existing user experience to meet the needs of these customers.

We iterated through several prototype user interfaces (wireframes of desktop and mobile web pages, then click-through mockups) with different options before their feedback told us which design to work with. We launched the overall software implementation project for Coca-Cola and stuck with our two-week agile sprint cadence. With each sprint, we were able to iterate versions of the desktop and mobile ordering experience software incorporating customer feedback until we reached a version that was ready to test with actual customers in the field. This field testing provided additional feedback that we incorporated prior to going live.

Hopefully these two examples helped to illustrate similarities and shared values between design thinking processes and agile. The examples from Promega and CloudCraze show how design thinking and agile practices combine to create successful products that solve real customer problems through innovative solutions.

Summary

Design thinking methods are highly supportive of and complementary to agile approaches to projects and product development. A hybrid approach to projects and products combining the elements of design thinking and agile allows people and organizations to learn about and focus on the needs of their customers, iterating through the design and development process through rapid prototyping. While sometimes referred to as "failing fast," this approach really means "getting something in front of the customer to react to and provide feedback."

The next chapter will discuss the unique role of the executive leader in agile environments and how the mindset and performance of this leader is extremely influential on the success of the methodology, the morale and performance of the teams, and the projects and products it is used to create and deliver.

The Executive Leader in Agile

Leading for success

As I wrote this book, I was working on my doctorate in leadership and working as the CIO at a technical college. As a consequence, I thought a lot about leadership and how senior leaders can influence the success or failure of agile within an organization. Aside from the various tactical challenges noted elsewhere in this book, the biggest causes of failed or muted agile are failures at the senior leadership level. These failures can manifest as failure to provide the appropriate support to the teams and the organization as they work to try agile or improve on it. The other way that senior leaders fail their teams and organizations is by failing to prioritize in the way that organizations, regardless of methodology, must do in order to run their project deliveries effectively and for maximum benefit to the organization.

The executive leader has a critical role in the adoption and implementation of agile practice within their organization. Like any change, the sustained and unequivocal support of leadership is among the most crucial success factors to an organization's attempts to adopt and use an agile framework to deliver projects and other work. For this reason, it is also critical for leaders to understand not only the necessity of their support for the overall adoption of

© Shawn Belling 2020
S. Belling, *Succeeding with Agile Hybrids*, https://doi.org/10.1007/978-1-4842-6461-4_11

agile but also how the decisions made by leaders become even more impactful given the reliance of agile on rapid decision-making to deliver value rapidly and continuously to their organization.

Executive leaders must recognize how their understanding of agile influences their decision-making and the impact their decisions and leadership have on the organization's ability to successfully leverage agile methods. An agile executive must understand how agile practices fit in organizational culture and structure and with other project management methods used in the organization. Recognition of misconceptions about agile, the need for rapid decisions, effective governance, removal of organizational impediments, and servant-leadership at the executive level will help the executive leader perform effectively in agile environments and ensure organizations maximize the potential benefits of agile.

Leadership Misconceptions of Agile

When executives learn about agile, it is not uncommon to learn about only the possible benefits of agile and misunderstand how these possible benefits are truly realized. These misconceptions happen when executives gain only a superficial understanding of agile methodologies and practices. The most common misconception is that agile equates to "faster," and that choosing to use agile on a specific project or as an approach to project management will automatically make projects complete faster than previously seen.

Other misconceptions include the assumption that agile project management will reduce the amount of planning necessary for successful projects or that projects could go faster because less documentation or measurement will be needed to be successful. It is also a misconception that agile project management is somehow less disciplined than traditional project management approaches.

Recognizing the common misconceptions helps the savvy executive recognize when their misconceptions of agile are affecting their leadership decisions while there is still time to correct the decision. One example of this misconception is assuming that the initial release plan generated by an agile team will be the plan followed throughout the duration of that project vs. recognizing that each sprint will result in some adjustment to the plan.

Leadership Mistakes with Agile

I've seen executives with only basic knowledge of agile methodologies and practices make assumptions about agile practices and misapply them. When this happens, the benefits of agile may not be realized, and the use of agile in the organization may be diminished or even fail. It is not uncommon for executives to assume that using agile means a project will be completed faster, or that less planning and discipline will be necessary. Executives may also misunderstand some metrics used with agile to the overall detriment of specific projects or the successful adoption and usage of the practices within their organizations.

While consulting for a health insurance company, I was in a project steering meeting and heard the CIO propose an agile approach for a project expecting that this would automatically shorten the overall projected duration of the project. I knew that the CIO's familiarity with agile practices was very basic, and that agile was not the best approach to use with the project in question. I also knew that this meeting was not the place to expose the CIO's basic understanding of agile. After the meeting, I met with the PMO leader (he was also in the meeting) to discuss and to propose a conversation with the CIO. The PMO leader met with the CIO to explain how agile does not equate to "faster" when looking at the overall duration of a project.

Here are a few other leadership mistakes I've personally witnessed and worked through:

- A vice president adding work from another project that was behind schedule into the backlog of an agile project and team in hopes that it would get done faster.

- Business and IT leadership forcing a team to co-locate into a "team room" in hopes that forced collaboration would "motivate" the team to complete their work sooner.

- A senior director at a client on one of my CloudCraze implementation projects asked the project team to add a second daily stand-up to their routine to review and report on bug status – resulting in less time each day to work on the bugs (on this one, the lead architect called me nearly in tears to ask me to talk the client out of this – I did).

- **Early days of CloudCraze** – Working with a vice president of product management who was not versed in the need to maintain a prioritized backlog of work, which caused sprint planning to be ineffective and the sprints to start late and underplanned.

- **All too common** – Spreading resources across multiple projects in an effort to make incremental progress on these projects.

When senior leaders believe or assume that "agile" means "faster," or that using agile practices will quickly fix long-standing system problems with project delivery, it often results in ineffective or failed agile projects and practices. Smart executives will seek education in agile methodologies to avoid these misconceptions. This education can help leaders avoid common mistakes and leadership failures that can have short- and long-term impacts within their organizations and result in diminished returns from the organization's investment in adoption of agile methodologies and practices.

How Executive Leadership Can Influence Agile's Benefits

Executive leaders in organizations that are using agile practices must understand how their leadership and decisions influence the outcomes. A savvy executive will recognize how timely decision-making and accountability can ensure that agile projects and teams in their purview maintain a high pace of output and high-quality deliverables. Executives who don't understand how their leadership could help maximize agile benefits put their organizations at risk of their agile teams and projects missing out the potential benefits of agile practices.

An organization, its projects, and employees realize the complete benefits of agile when agile practices are fully implemented and leveraged within an organization. As noted earlier – with any change or process improvement, the most critical success factor is executive buy-in and support. It's also key for executives to recognize how their decisions help to focus their organizations on projects that deliver the highest value to their customers. They in turn must hold their product owners, scrum masters, and project teams accountable for value creation while holding themselves accountable for providing timely guidance and governance.

Executives have a different type of responsibility in agile environments. They set an example by holding themselves and their peers accountable for the same behaviors that help agile teams function. Leadership teams get pulled in many directions each day, but they can support their agile teams and projects by meeting daily to make decisions needed to keep the teams and projects moving and then communicating these decisions quickly.

Don't Create Impediments – Remove Them

Leaders in agile environments best serve the organization when they are removing impediments, but sometimes the executives are an impediment. Avoiding situations where executives slow down agile teams is critical. Conversely, being attuned to impediment removal is also critical. Jeff

Sutherland once said, "For Scrum to really take off, someone in senior management needs to understand in his bones that impediments are nearly criminal. The effect of eliminating waste is dramatic, but people often don't do it, because it requires being honest with themselves and with other."

Earlier, I noted how a senior director created an impediment by asking for a second daily stand-up focused on bug status – major impediment. Another impediment that senior leaders sometimes create is by insisting on showing up at team's daily stand-ups. Even if they manage to remain silent, they still create an impediment for the team just by being present. The muting effect that senior leaders have on their team's ability to communicate candidly with each other cannot be underestimated.

One of the most important contributions of an executive in an agile environment is to remove impediments that a team cannot remove because it lacks authority. The impediment could involve a spend approval or an organizational change that the executive would need to sponsor and approve. For example – at CloudCraze, as the breadth and complexity of the overall product expanded, it became increasingly clear that the development organization's ability to rapidly and thoroughly test the software due to lack of automated testing tools was severely limiting the team's capacity in sprints and releases.

The QA manager regularly brought this to my attention, and I stepped up the pressure on our new owners to approve the funding necessary to acquire these tools. I recall one of the tipping points being my use of a well-placed F-bomb to describe our lack of automated testing as "f***ing embarrassing." Given that I rarely curse (at least in professional settings), this helped to convey the seriousness of the situation and the urgency of remedying it as quickly as possible.

My agile coach/scrum master and I removed another impediment when we made the decision to split our single large development team into two smaller teams. Over time, the team had grown to the point that sprint planning and daily stand-ups (performed virtually through conference calls) were becoming inefficient. The team had not wanted to make this change; however, the scrum master/agile coach and I knew it was the right move. I had to own and make this tough decision.

When agile leaders act and are accountable to each other and their teams to help realize these benefits through actions such as timely decision-making, it maximizes these benefits for the whole organization. Executives must be aware of scenarios where their actions or failure to act could actually impede agile teams and projects and learn how to avoid those situations. An executive should remove organizational impediments allowing the teams to work more efficiently and maximize value creation.

Ruthless Prioritization

One of the soapboxes I've chosen to stand on throughout my career is the importance of prioritization in project management. I've seen otherwise respected and successful organizations struggle with projects because they could not or chose not to do the hard work of prioritization. In environments where everything is top priority, nothing is top priority. A key responsibility of senior leadership is ruthless prioritization, leaving no doubt as to the organization's top projects.

There are four common scenarios where failure to ruthlessly prioritize impedes project execution. While these scenarios transcend any project management approach, they are even more impactful when an organization is using agile practices.

The compromise – The compromise scenario comes from fear of slowing some "important" projects in favor of other projects and pushes leaders to a poor compromise. No tough decisions are made, no projects are paused or deprived of resources, and all projects continue. Resources are diluted and spread thinly across these projects, reducing progress to a crawl.

By prioritizing too many things, the organization makes minimal progress on many projects, but makes no value-creating progress on any. Compromising on prioritization also compromises competitive advantage.

Do it all – This scenario asks teams and resources to work 80-hour weeks to make measurable progress on multiple "priority" projects. Sometimes this is necessary in early phases of startups, and rare "bet the company" scenarios where this approach is warranted for a short, intense time.

Too often, the 80-hour-week solution is senior leaders' failure to prioritize vital few projects, combined with willingness to place the burden of failure to prioritize on their teams and resources. In the short term, this tactic can yield results. Beyond a few months, any accelerated value delivery is unsustainable. Long term, this tactic burns out teams, creates toxic workplaces, and causes turnover.

Analysis paralysis – Slightly less destructive is the analysis paralysis scenario. This emerges when the organization's senior leaders have low urgency to prioritize and direct project teams and resources accordingly. Instead, their repeated requests for "what-ifs" burn cycles from key resources, create zero value, and create a false impression of careful consideration while concealing indecisiveness.

Organizations afflicted with analysis paralysis can't advance their key projects. Team morale suffers as they perform low-value work while developing scenarios for consideration at the next project review meeting. When a decision is finally made, too much time has been lost and effort wasted that could have been saved by decisive leadership through ruthless prioritization.

All projects are high priority – Worst-case scenario: senior leaders telling subordinates to treat everything as top priority and "find a way." Prioritization is not easy. Senior leaders put their reputation, credibility, and even their career on the line with these decisions. This partially justifies their compensation and perqs. The expectation is leaders know their business, strategy, and teams and therefore can make these tough calls. That is why it is unacceptable to pass tough priority decisions and consequences to subordinates when senior leaders are literally paid to prioritize.

Avoiding these problem scenarios requires a regular and ruthless prioritization process for projects. This seems obvious, but many organizations lack this or the ability to execute it at critical times. Like security or disaster planning, ruthless and rigorous prioritization cannot be reactive or situational. It must be become as routine and natural as coming to work and becomes easier to sustain over time. In organizations where this is the norm, any pause or deviation from this cadence is impactful. The organization comes to rely on the process, even take it for granted. This is a good thing – it means everyone at all levels is bought in, the rhythm is there, and it is a natural business process.

The challenge is getting this in place. Like all change, it requires realization of the problem and the importance of fixing it. Once an organization follows through on the commitment to put a rigorous prioritization process in place, they must stick to it every week. From the CEO down, there must be an environment of accountability and rigor in assessing priorities and recognition of the critical role of constrained resources as engines of value creation. They can be driven hard, but selectively, and only when priorities support this, lest you burn them out.

Ruthless prioritization means having a vital few projects with senior leaders accountable for ranking them and acting accordingly. It means senior leaders are willing to make and have the data and process to support decisions such as:

- Pulling resources off an important project and dealing with the fallout in order to execute on a more important project

- Delaying or canceling "nice to have" projects that please some stakeholders but create little or no value or competitive advantage

- Stopping some projects to take advantage of a window of opportunity and accept that a near-complete product release might slip

- Appeasing an angry customer for one more sprint in order to ship a near-complete product release or – the exact opposite – delay the release to fix the angry customer situation

Finally, it means scrutinizing the project and product portfolio every two to four weeks without fail and revisiting decisions if new or changed conditions warrant. This requires a structured agile governance process. I've put this in place in some organizations and coached other organizations on how to stand it up and operate it. I do not claim this to be the best or most perfect approach to agile governance, but it's worked for me.

Agile Governance

Executive leaders are responsible for governing projects, project portfolios, and products in their organizations. Executives are responsible for evaluating projects and new product development efforts before they are started to ensure they are a good fit for the organization and its objectives. They must evaluate results and metrics to ensure that the projects are progressing and will deliver expected value.

Agile requires a continuous focus on governance and decision-making from executives due in part to agile's rapid iterative pace. Agile projects will stall or see their value delivery muted if executive leaders do not provide continuous input and timely decisions, particularly associated with prioritization.

The biggest difference between agile project governance and governance in plan-driven project environments is the pace and frequency at which governance input is needed. Executives accustomed to phase-based project environments may expect monthly steering committee meetings where project decisions are debated or deferred for further consideration. Environments and approaches like this will stifle agile projects and cause them to stall, fail, and ultimately prevent them from delivering value to the organization.

Using Metrics for Agile Governance

Executives operating in agile environments should expect to see frequent updates from various project, product, and value stream efforts within their organizations. The agile teams work from roadmaps defined by organizational strategies and objectives which are set by executive leadership. The path to progress toward these objectives is mapped out in release plans which are then executed by the various teams in their sprints.

The executive leadership team brings important information and perspectives to the governance process. Input from the executives representing sales, various customer-facing operations such as implementation or customer success, product support, and product management must all be considered and balanced to provide guidance to the agile teams and projects. Based on this input and the evaluation, the executive leadership team may adjust the overall objectives of the release plans and sprints to meet the evolving needs of the organization.

Making Leadership Decisions in Agile Environments

Executive leadership and project governance imply making decisions that are sometimes challenging or unpopular. In agile environments, these decisions must be made rapidly so that the agile teams are not waiting for direction or impediment removal.

Executives are called upon to guide projects and project teams based on the information they receive and the outcomes of the ongoing sprints and releases. They must consider the likelihood of completing committed features in a release along with the risks that technical or resource challenges are posing. Executives must provide guidance and decisions on whether at-risk features or deliverables should be dropped or deferred, or whether less-vital features should be dropped to focus on must-have features.

Leaders must also consider external factors such as customer requests, input from sales, movements in the competitive landscape, and important customer-facing projects or implementations that may be dependent on or influenced by the deliverables from ongoing agile projects. These external factors combined with the progress of projects and teams influence the guidance and decisions that executives are called upon to make to govern the projects or products and keep the overall flow of agile projects moving so that the organization regularly realizes value from them.

Executive Servant-Leadership in Agile

Servant-leadership is a core tenet of agile project management practices. At the project team level, scrum masters/agile project managers are expected to be effective servant-leaders. At the executive level, effective servant-leadership is even more important, because it sets the tone for the organization and ensures that leaders are focused on empowering their project teams, providing timely decisions, removing any impediments to their progress, and ensuring they have the resources they need to deliver value to the organization. This enables the organization to leverage the benefits of the agile methodologies.

Executives used to more formal or traditional management structures must recognize that in agile, the effective leader works in service to the people in the organization that can deliver value. An executive leader in the contemporary business environment embraces the evolution away from the bureaucratic, status-conscious hierarchical structure and toward the flatter, leaner organization focused on merit and value creation. An executive servant-leader recognizes that empowered teams working in agile environments need leaders who will protect them and do whatever must be done to enable them to work effectively with focus on the customer.

Impacts of Missing Servant-Leadership

Successful use of agile practices to deliver value requires that everyone in the organization be accountable to keep things moving. When executive leaders fail to do this, the processes break down. Agile teams cannot be effective without governance, prioritization, continuous feedback and strategic direction, and constant attention to removing organizational impediments.

Executives who are invested in hierarchy versus value creation will cause agile teams and projects to slow down, ultimately becoming impediments to value delivery. Executives who fail to hold themselves and their peers accountable to do whatever must be done to enable agile to work in the organization do a disservice to their customers and their teams. Agile leaders who don't participate in sprint reviews and ask what they can do to help teams improve performance are not helping their people, teams, and organization become iteratively more productive through agile practices.

Executives who expect use of agile practices to "fix" projects, make projects "go faster," or who somehow expect to reap the benefits of agile practices without investing in them, changing the culture, or changing their own behavior are ultimately responsible for failed agile projects and implementations. Executives who embody servant-leadership enable their organizations to leverage benefits of agile. An executive servant-leader should work to empower teams by providing necessary guidance and resources and also by removing obstacles that can hinder value delivery.

Summary

Executive leadership sets the tone for success or failure in agile environments. Creating a culture of accountability, timely decision-making, support for prioritization, and servant-leadership helps to foster environments where agile and agile hybrids have a higher chance for success. Executives who cannot or choose not to lead in this way are doing their organizations, their projects, and their people a serious disservice. Agile is all about value delivery, and the effective agile executive does everything possible to ensure that their leadership removes impediments and creates opportunities for rapid value realization through agile.

In the next chapter, we discuss approaches to implementing agile practices. We will discuss approaches and impediments to implementing agile as well as review questions that should be asked to determine if an organization is ready to start using agile or an agile hybrid.

Implementing Agile

Giving agile a try

(**Author's note:** The reader will notice that most of the material in Chapter 12 has also appeared in Chapter 2. This is intentional, to ensure that users of this text in academic or training settings can assign this chapter as standalone reading where necessary.) The most successful implementations of agile are often when a small group of practitioners just decide to go for it. Whether they have used it elsewhere and want to bring it to their new organization, have heard about it and want to try, whatever – the grassroots interest and enthusiasm of a group of people who think they can improve their ways of working cannot be matched as a foundation for success. That's how it was for us at Promega when the .NEXT team decided to try FDD and then extended our use of agile as we learned more.

Other scenarios involve senior management decisions to use agile on specific projects or within specific parts of an organization, and essentially telling a working team or group that they will start using Agile. This can potentially go well, or could be disastrous, depending on the circumstances. Attempting to use agile on a project for which an agile framework is not a good fit or jamming agile practices into an environment where people are not ready or the culture poses challenges are almost certain to result in poor outcomes and a negative view of agile as an approach to project management.

© Shawn Belling 2020
S. Belling, *Succeeding with Agile Hybrids*, https://doi.org/10.1007/978-1-4842-6461-4_12

Assessing Projects

There are a number of things to consider when you're evaluating what approach – agile or a traditional plan-driven approach – may be best for a type of project. In a plan-driven or waterfall scenario, the environment is assumed to be predictable – we assume that there's a tendency toward stability and a way of thinking in terms of projects that deal in concrete, brick, steel, glass. Things are going to be built once and then remain the same for a very long period of time – a long service life, like with a building, a ship, or a power plant.

These targets tend to be stationary – we know what it is we are trying to achieve at the outset and then we note that target is not going to change. In fact, change is bad, and allowing change in the context of the project could be damaging. We have an assumption that the work can be directed. We have to consider it the way that we would consider firing a bullet – once we release that work, we are not going to be able to really guide it on a trajectory, but rather we have to be certain as we start the work that is going to achieve outcomes, so we aim carefully before we release.

We seek all of our strategic input at the very start of the project given some of these other factors, and therefore that drives a highly detailed plan to enable us to achieve that stationary target. In projects that are suitable for the plan-driven or waterfall approach, there is usually an understanding that we gain economies of scale as we go with larger and larger projects, and that we get some economy of scale as we release large increments of the project. We have a strong emphasis on control, on managing all the outcomes, on trying to stick to the plan and assessing our progress and adjusting to closely follow that plan to achieve our goals.

Agile projects assume some different things. We assume that our outcomes may be difficult to predict because rapid change is the norm, as is often the case in an environment like high technology, software development, biological research, and life sciences, where we may see weekly change. This type of environment lends itself to getting value from agile project approaches – the targets are moving. Change is good, and the impact, if we resist change, could be damaging to the outcome of our project.

Once the work is started in an agile environment, the assumption is that we can guide this work, much like one can guide a missile in flight. You launch the missile, you launch the work, but then you can make course corrections to ensure that you achieve the desired outcome. We seek strategic input throughout the entire project life cycle – it's not something that needs to be given upfront and then ideally does not change, but rather something we seek constantly to ensure that we are on the right track.

Rapid feedback enables us to stay close to hitting the moving target (like that gazelle being chased by the cheetah) that may very well be the strategic objectives associated with this project. We can keep it relevant in the situation by doing rapid iterative releases so that the value can be assessed and aligned with ongoing strategic objectives. We use adaptation to achieve our goals and therefore we give up some degree of control in favor of that adaptation.

Environment is predictable; stability is norm; concrete/steel/glass – same for decades = waterfall	Environment difficult to predict; rapid change is norm. High-tech; weekly change = agile > Scrum?
Stationary targets	Moving targets
Change is bad; allowing it is damaging	Change is good, resisting change is damaging
Work directable, like a bullet – aim, aim, fire	Work is guidable like a missile in flight – course corrections, aim, fire, aim
Strategic input needed at start	Strategic input needed throughout
Detailed plan – stationary target	Rapid feedback – moving target
Gain economies of scale with size	Achieve relevance with quick iterative releases
Emphasis on control to achieve goals	Emphasis on adaptation to achieve goals – give up some control

Figure 12-1. Comparing project environments – adapted from Collyer, Warren, Helmsley, and Stevens, 2010, p. 116

Assessing the Organization

In 2011, a question that I asked in class was "is your organization ready to adopt agile as a project management approach?". As I write in 2020, it's perhaps more appropriate to ask, "why wouldn't your organization be ready to become more agile?" Throughout the 2010s, *Harvard Business Review* (HBR) published a series of articles on agile practices in business (recall HBR is where Scrum first appeared in the Takeuchi and Nonaka article in 1986). These articles (many coauthored by Jeff Sutherland as well as Hirohito Takeuchi) examined the increasing adoption of agile practices and discussed both cautionary perspectives and advocating for the adoption of agile practices. The new buzz phrase that I see everywhere is "organizational agility".

Agile methodologies have moved out of new product development and software development into many other verticals and organizational types. Organizations as diverse as John Deere (farming equipment), National Public Radio (public radio), Saab (fighter jets), and a winery are just a few examples of organizations that have adopted Agile practices in some form to improve their management and operations and get people out of their functional silos and into new and different ways of thinking (Rigby, Sutherland & Takeuchi, 2016).

You must assess whether your organization is in a good position to make the transition to an agile project management approach. There are a number of areas that should be considered and evaluated as you consider introducing this approach to project management. A thorough, honest, and realistic appraisal of your organization can give you a sense of the size of the hill you are about to climb.

Start by considering your organizational culture. Culture is a complex and multilayered element in this discussion, but one important and obvious consideration is the culture's willingness to accept or tolerate change. Change is never easy, but organizations with a culture that is especially resistant to change, or that has had difficulty with change in the past, may find adoption of agile approaches to project management especially difficult.

Organizations that operate in highly regulated industries may find agile does not suit or support their other processes or provide a level of comfort comparable to plan-driven project management approaches. That said, there are practitioners who have implemented agile in regulated environments with appropriate focus on testing and validation processes. In fact, it is in organizations like these where hybrid approaches can work well, mixing elements of plan-driven and agile project management to achieve desired results.

Multitiered and highly bureaucratic organizations are likely to find adoption of agile more challenging than flatter organizations with less bureaucracy. The constant and generally informal communications processes inherent in agile come more naturally to the flatter organizations that have already streamlined their processes and trimmed or avoided bureaucracies.

Take a hard look at your middle management. As organizations grow and mature, it is common to see the growth of middle management layers. It is quite common to see middle managers develop a tendency to focus on defining and protecting their turf or fiefdoms, and these organizations have to address these problems, ideally before considering a methodology that will expose these types of organizational dysfunctions.

Bureaucracies and middle management fiefdoms sound fairly daunting, but given where I am based (Madison, WI), many of the organizations I have done agile training and coaching for are state government agencies and the IT department of our flagship state university, as well as within the large insurance companies that are fixtures around Madison. These organizations decided it was worth the effort to try to adopt agile practices to improve their project delivery and operational execution.

Critical Success Factors

As with any change initiative, there are critical factors that can help increase the odds that experimentation and adoption of agile can be successful. The support and buy-in of the organization's senior leaders are critical, as with any initiative. Cultivation of respected evangelists in the organization who are willing and able to generate interest and support from peers in the organization will help, as will lining up some smaller projects with which to get some quick wins early in the adoption process.

Once the organization decides to go further with agile, it is important to plan for and invest in good training. This lays a solid foundation of common practices and brings most of the organization in at the same level. Developing and training internal experts combined with solid externally sourced training helps ensure that the organization is well positioned to implement agile, as well as develop good processes to support the implementation.

Tips for Successful Implementation

- Leadership buy-in and support
- Evangelists
- Some small, quick wins – start small, evaluate, adapt
- Good training – common training
- Build good processes

Brian Rabon (n.d.) describes some additional ideas for implementing agile project management. Rabon notes that easing into adoption and being pragmatic in one's approach is key. Rabon notes that not every aspect of a methodology should be dogmatically implemented, because (as noted previously) company history and culture has a significant impact. The need to embrace change as part of agile is key – a fundamental part of using agile is accepting change. This does not mean abandoning change management, but rather accepting the more flexible perspective that agile brings to change within projects.

Rabon reinforces servant-leadership as an important element. As we've discussed previously, servant-leadership is key for the scrum master/agile PM and senior leaders working in agile environments. Rabon reminds us that being a project manager in agile means it is about the team, and that command-and-control methods will not work. Lastly, Rabon suggests finding a good project or customer as a candidate for piloting agile practices. The project might be a small, less-visible project, but the customer should be one that is willing and able to be fully engaged in the ongoing involvement needed throughout the agile project life cycle (Rabon, n.d.).

A common practice when trying new ways of doing things is to do so on low-stakes or under the radar projects. That way, those interested in experimenting with a new approach (Linux servers, agile development, remote work, flex hours, etc.) can see what works and doesn't work prior to publicizing their experiment. In this way, a small group of practitioners in an organization can try out some practical elements of agile to see how they work in their setting. As a trainer, consultant, and leader, I encourage and support this practice because I have seen it work multiple times, and because the alternative (doing things the same old way) is increasingly unacceptable even while attempting massive change may be too big of a hill to climb all at once.

Practical Examples

I've discussed my early experiences with agile at Promega Corporation elsewhere in this book. In 2009, a new senior leader (Kari) joined Promega with executive oversight of both marketing and IT. Kari had come from a successful career at a regional consulting firm where she grew the business by implementing ecommerce projects using agile practices. Joining Promega, she found a small but enthusiastic group of evangelists willing to embrace and grow some of the agile experiments we'd already tried. Kari brought in some trusted consultants as well as invested in training to help extend the interest and capabilities, and we began to use agile practice more – not only on IT projects but on cross-functional marketing and IT projects as well.

At CloudCraze, I joined a small product development team attempting to use agile (Scrum) led by a VP who was also sold on the necessity to use agile for our software development endeavors. Coming in with training and experience as well as credibility in that I had begun to teach and train for the University of Wisconsin, the leadership team embraced and supported ongoing learning and adoption of Scrum – not only for product development but for our customer-facing software implementation projects as well.

While consulting for a large health insurance company, I was asked to spin up and lead a provider web portal enhancement project on which the company wanted to try agile for various reasons. Despite the challenges present in the scenario (which I describe earlier in the book), the endeavor did have the support of senior leadership. The company also accepted my offer of some short, semiformal agile orientation sessions to generate some basic awareness of agile within the organization. Agile definitely took off there – after I completed my assignment and left for my current CIO role, the company did a major reorganization of their PMO and their IT department and launched an agile transformation program.

Typical Impediments

There are challenges typical to the adoption and implementation of agile in many organizations. It's become widely accepted that rigorous implementation of agile will reveal or highlight problems in other areas – one thing I like to say is that there is nowhere to hide on an agile team, and the same is true in an agile organization.

Often, the challenges are with management or at the organizational level. Many senior leaders think that agile is a quick or magic fix and therefore expect to see the benefits from agile without making real changes in supporting business processes and philosophies. As we discussed in a previous chapter, senior leaders must be part of the change and must in fact be the removers of impediments at the leadership and organizational level.

At the functional level, there are plenty of obstacles as well. Too often, team members, especially those who feel that they don't really need to be in every daily stand-up meeting, find reasons not to attend, and soon the value of their involvement is lost along with the expectation. Along these same lines, the stand-ups themselves may be poorly run, or run in an undisciplined way that diminishes their value and makes people not want to participate.

Team members also may resist some of the other changes in routines that come with best practice implementation of agile, such as co-location and ready accessibility. The collaborative team work and accountability required for successful agile can be an issue for people who see themselves as above their peers. As well, some people just don't want to give up their private offices or other perqs of their positions for the relative equality of an agile team.

Agile relies on constant direction and involvement from product owners, and many times the people who are in this role are people who are, or choose to be, too busy to provide the close engagement and involvement required to be a strong product owner. It may also be that they may not be willing or able to make the tough decisions needed to regularly prioritize a backlog of features that can't all be realized in a single project or release.

Another impediment emerges when managers use the metrics generated in agile to put pressure on the team. Instead of using velocity as a measure of sustainable performance and throughput, they pressure the team to work faster or take on larger commitments.

Additional challenges come when one area in an organization such as IT or product development chooses to adopt agile while the remainder of the organization retains other methods for managing projects. Elsewhere in the book, we've talked about the encouraging trend from the late 2010s into 2020 showing that embracing agility throughout organizations is gaining traction, so hopefully this impediment decreases in frequency.

In software development, a challenge comes in the change of mindset from project-based software delivery to an ongoing, sustained delivery model in which a team can maintain a pace of regular value-adding releases. Generally speaking, the change in mindset from getting all features, benefits, and value all at once at the end of a long project can be a problem for organizations – they cannot adapt to the roadmap approach in which prioritized business value is delivered incrementally and ongoing.

The ownership of the product owner role can be a challenge in some organizations. It requires hard choices and discipline to constantly assess the value of the product backlog and accept that you can have some things now and some things in later releases.

Organizations that see their Agile implementations fail or become muted often do so because the people attempting to implement agile ultimately give in to the resistance of the culture and dysfunctional elements. Influential people in the organization, often people who are fearful, resistant or skeptical of any type of project management use this influence to undermine the adoption for fear of the change it may effect or out of impatience or lack of appreciation for the value it could bring. The challenges noted here are where an agile coach can be extremely valuable in reminding an organization why they started with agile and helping them to assess how to get the adoption and implementation on track.

It's important to ensure that everyone in the organization understands that agile does not equate to immediate faster delivery. It is also important to note that at times, changes identified by the teams may slow them down temporarily. I've offered the advice and observation that teams would need to slow down in order to go faster many times. Tommy Norman, a Lean/Agile coach, notes:

> *Be careful promising your stakeholders that moving to Agile will increase delivery speed right out of the gate. Methods like Scrum and Kanban help to quickly expose issues around delivery, but they don't fix them. When you first adopt Agile, you will be presented with these opportunities to address your issues, but that takes time and experimentation. Initially you might actually be SLOWER until you can address the right issues. If people come into Agile thinking that at the end of your first Sprint there will be some significant increase in productivity, they might be disappointed and start to think Agile is the problem. Set expectations appropriately and help people learn to see the value in exposing and addressing underlying issues. Show them the value in slowing down to speed up.*
> (Norman, 2019)

Summary

Implementing agile can take many forms. Whether a grassroots initiative or a top-down decision from leadership, implementing agile practices comes with many challenges and potential impediments. Organizational culture, as with any other significant change, tends to be the largest obstacle to successful adoption of agile or hybrid agile practices. We have discussed several ways to prepare to attempt agile and identified elements of the organization you should know about as you consider whether agile is a fit for your project or for your organization.

In the next chapter, we discuss approaches to scaling agile practices. We will discuss approaches and impediments to implementing agile as well as review questions that should be asked to determine if an organization is ready to start using agile or an agile hybrid.

Approaches to Scaling Agile

Determining when and how to scale

The evolution of agile approaches to projects and other organizational endeavors brought with it the emergence of approaches to scaling agile. My intent in the overview and discussion that follows here is to provide exactly that – overview and discussion. I'm focusing on three approaches to scaling agile, specifically Scrum, that are relatively well known. There are three main approaches to scaling agile that are particularly important to know – Large-Scale Scrum (LeSS), Scaled Agile Framework (SAFe), and Scrum@Scale.

Understanding the key components and being aware of the pros and cons of each of these approaches can help practitioners and their organizations select and implement the scaling approach that could work best for your organization and scenarios. Understanding the key elements of each will also help the practitioner working within organizations that are implementing or already have implemented one of these three frameworks.

Each of these approaches to scaling agile has strengths and weaknesses depending on your particular situation. They are also detailed and substantial on their own and are best enjoyed after the practitioner develops a strong foundation in agile frameworks – in the case of LeSS and Scrum@Scale,

© Shawn Belling 2020

S. Belling, *Succeeding with Agile Hybrids*, https://doi.org/10.1007/978-1-4842-6461-4_13

particularly Scrum. I recommend that a practitioner interested in learning more about one or more of these approaches do some reading and get some hands-on training after developing that foundation in agile and scrum.

Large-Scale Scrum (LeSS)

LeSS was developed by Craig Larman and Bas Vodde in 2005. It deliberately leverages the core elements of Scrum that define how a single team uses Scrum to deliver a potentially shippable increment of a product during each sprint and scales them to work across multiple teams. Larman and Vodde have a fine book on LeSS called *Large-Scale Scrum: More with LeSS* in which they detail the practices and philosophies behind LeSS. Much of this section is based on my reading of their book.

LeSS provides a framework for multiple teams to leverage Scrum and work together to create completed work elements and then contribute these multiple elements to a single shippable product. For example, two or three Scrum teams could use LeSS to coordinate, combine, and deliver features to a single software product, either in a release or through continuous delivery.

According to Larman and Vodde, in the LeSS framework, large can mean up to as many as five teams, possibly working at one or two locations. Scenarios in which a LeSS framework is being considered for hundreds of teams and overall larger scenarios where these teams could span multiple locations are referred to as LeSS Huge (Larman & Vodde, 2016).

Key Practices of LeSS

In terms of Scrum and agile elements, LeSS

- Uses the core practices of Scrum as is and applies them to larger scenarios and should not be misinterpreted as a new or improved version of Scrum.

- Does not introduce new roles, artifacts, or processes to the basic Scrum framework. LeSS retains Scrum's focus on self-managed and highly accountable teams leveraging the Scrum framework.

- Offers constant and iterative improvement. Like Scrum, it leverages the ongoing and evolutionary cycle of learning to improve the product and the team's practices.

- Uses a plan-do-check-act cycle to constantly strive toward creating better products, faster, less expensively, with high quality, while meeting the needs of customers.

- Uses lean approaches such as managers as teachers, respect for people, seeking to improve, and fixing defects as they are found (Larman & Vodde, 2016).

Product and Process Focus

In terms of product and process focus to scale, LeSS

- Relies on transparency through truly done work products, short time-boxed iterations, teamwork, and an environment where experiments are encouraged and mistakes are not punished.

- Focuses on the entire product, that is, there is a single backlog, product owner (PO), product, and sprint regardless of the number of teams.

- Focuses on determining the value customers need to receive through solved problems, as with Scrum.

- Incorporates systems thinking and requires an understanding of and focus on the entire system with an eye toward optimization of the system as a whole, as opposed to any specific subcomponent or individual.

- Relies on empirical data to evaluate and control the process. It relies on the actual outcomes from every sprint to determine how to adjust and improve processes and the product.

- Requires an understanding of how queued processes work in scenarios where research and development is being performed and how to account for the limits of work in progress and the size of the work components (Larman & Vodde, 2016).

Practices That Are Important to Success with LeSS

There are some LeSS practices that are critical to successfully using LeSS to scale agile and scrum. For example, LeSS relies on a full-time scrum master (SM) to work across the LeSS teams. Like Scrum, LeSS functions best when the performing organization commits to having long-lived teams.

It is most effective when the teams are co-located rather than teams being distributed. This does not mean distributed teams cannot work, but co-location is preferred. LeSS relies on independent teams working on a single goal without relying on direction from a program or portfolio pushing work down to the teams. LeSS requires cross-functional teams and does not rely on shared services such as separate integration or architectural teams. In LeSS, these shared services slow teams down. Manager roles exist in LeSS purely to ensure teams have resources and learning that they need to be successful, and not to dictate how the teams perform their work (Larman & Vodde, 2016).

When to Use LeSS

LeSS works best when applied to a single product because the framework assumes a single PO, a single backlog, one scrum master working across the teams, and one sprint and release cadence that multiple teams will use. Multiple products and multiple backlogs indicate a scenario where basic LeSS is not the best approach.

For example, a software company with a single product and one team that has grown too large to effectively use basic Scrum would use LeSS as follows: They would maintain a single product backlog managed by a single PO. It would maintain one sprint and release cadence rather than allowing the teams to operate on different cadences. One scrum master would work with the two or perhaps three newly formed teams to help them leverage Scrum and LeSS effectively.

Scaled Agile Framework (SAFe)

SAFe is a framework of processes that can help larger organizations scale agile practices. SAFe considers the needs and special challenges faced by larger organizations as they seek to scale agile over multiple products, portfolios, programs, workstreams, and teams. SAFe is more complex and adds more roles and structure as compared to Large-Scale Scrum (LeSS) or Scrum@ Scale.

The origins and development of the foundations of SAFe are credited to Dean Leffingwell, who founded and leads a company that owns and provides the SAFe content. Much of this section is based on my reading and review of SAFe materials in order to evaluate it for my own understanding as well as to teach about it at an awareness level in my courses. It is a substantial framework, and those seeking to use it should seek additional information and perhaps one of the SAFe certifications that are available.

Key Practices of SAFe

At its foundation, SAFe is based on the core tenets of agile, lean product development, and systems thinking. SAFe itself has four core values, which are alignment, built-in quality, transparency, and program execution.

Alignment refers to the alignment of the company at its strategic product and portfolio levels. This ensures that lower levels of the framework, most critically the product owners (POs), understand the strategic direction of the organization and make informed decisions and provide guidance to teams based on this alignment.

Built-in quality is a core tenet of agile practices. With SAFe, having quality built in to all processes, from architecture to design and development, is especially important. As an organization scales, the opportunities for quality issues to impact multiple elements of a product, program, or portfolio are multiplied.

Next, transparency means that, as with all agile practices, all information regarding priorities, progress, improvement opportunities, portfolio and program objectives, and strategies are visible to all.

Finally, program execution ensures that agile teams are indeed executing and delivering at a coordinated program level. Organizations often begin with individual agile teams but are challenged in scaling these up in a coordinated way ("Scaled Agile Framework – SAFe for lean enterprises," n.d.).

Core Competencies of SAFe

The core values of SAFe are supplemented by core competencies that can help to make SAFe a successful approach. These core competencies are lean-agile leadership, team and technical agility, development operations (DevOps) and release on demand, business solutions and lean systems engineering, and lean portfolio management.

Lean-agile leadership refers to the responsibility of the organization's leaders to create the environment and drive the changes in which SAFe can succeed by leveraging lean and agile leadership practices and values.

Team and technical agility are the ability of the organization's teams and their technical practices to use various agile practices and methods to consistently deliver their work in sprints while coordinating with other teams. In SAFe, this framework is called the agile release train (ART) where work is delivered by individual teams, coordinating with each other and contributing to the larger whole.

DevOps and release on demand are technical capabilities that are necessary for an organization to use SAFe effectively and maximize rapid value delivery. DevOps is an organizational mindset and technical framework that aligns development, production, security, and business operations processes. This, in turn, enables an organization using agile and SAFe practices and ART to be able to release working software at any time in the cycle, thereby delivering value as rapidly as possible.

SAFe is used by large organizations to deliver large and complex solutions and systems. Despite the size and complexity of these solutions, SAFe uses lean systems engineering and agile practices to design and build incrementally, avoiding large planning efforts and phase gates. Instead, it focuses on delivering value while retaining flexibility to learn and adapt.

The same lean and adaptive principles used to deliver large technical solutions in a coordinated way are also applied to the management of the portfolios to ensure investment decisions that support maximum value to the organization, whether to customer-facing products or to internal business process that in turn support the goal of value delivery to customers ("Scaled Agile Framework – SAFe for lean enterprises," n.d.).

How to Determine If SAFe Fits

SAFe is designed for larger organizations that must scale agile practices across multiple products, programs, and portfolios. SAFe assumes or requires the presence of supporting structures such as automated testing and deployment systems, architectural roadmaps and runways, and various shared services necessary to support multiple ARTs and value streams.

SAFe is a good choice for larger enterprises with more than 500 people and potentially hundreds of teams that have already achieved scale in their business operations and want to move their enterprise to more efficient and effective models of agile delivery at that scale.

SAFe is not a good choice for smaller organizations, startups, or organizations that do not have or do not need the level and scale of management structure that SAFe requires or implies.

Scrum@Scale

I attended Scrum@Scale practitioner training in 2018. I wanted to get formal training in one of the scaled approaches to Scrum, and it was also a great opportunity to learn directly from Scrum co-creator Dr. Jeff Sutherland. This section draws heavily on my training and the related materials as well as the Scrum@Scale website.

Scrum@Scale is an approach to scaling Scrum developed by Dr. Jeff Sutherland, the co-creator of Scrum. Sutherland has been scaling Scrum since the mid-1990s and introduced Scrum@Scale as the logical extension of core Scrum practices to scaled scenarios. Based on my in-class questions, Sutherland states that he also introduced Scrum@Scale in response to shortcomings he believes are present in LeSS and SAFe (Sutherland, J. Personal communication, July 2018).

Scrum@Scale is a framework in which coordinated Scrum teams can scale to address complex scenarios and deliver products and solutions of high value, whether these are software, hardware, systems, or services. Scrum@Scale uses the kind of scale-free architecture often found in biology, such as neural networks, to enable organizations to effectively coordinate an unlimited number of Scrum teams (Sutherland, 2018).

Scrum@Scale Practices

For its foundation, Scrum@Scale requires consistent and effective use of basic Scrum processes as prescribed by the *Scrum Guide*. Scrum@Scale leverages proper execution of these practices and uses the framework to coordinate and scale across teams, constantly improve and remove impediments, ensure ongoing prioritization and planning, ensure constant transparency to metrics, and enable regular delivery of value through potentially shippable increments of product.

Scrum@Scale focuses on two of the core roles of Scrum – the scrum master (SM) and the product owner (PO) – and their cycle of work and services to the Scrum teams. The Scrum@Scale framework applies the natural cycle of these roles and scales them organically to coordinate the activities of multiple scrum teams.

One of the core tenets of Scrum@Scale is the comparison to the traits of a cellular organism to describe its scale-free architecture. Much like a single cell in an organism contains all the specific processes for that cell and interacts with other cells to grow and create a larger organism, Scrum@Scale Scrum teams contain specific processes and leverage the framework to scale these processes (Sutherland, 2018).

Key Practices of Scrum@Scale

To understand Scrum@Scale, it is important to first know and understand the function and responsibilities of the Scrum team, SM, and the PO. The Scrum@Scale framework uses these core functions and responsibilities, assumes strong competencies in these roles, and then scales them. Some of the key elements of Scrum@Scale are the following:

- **Scrum of Scrums (SoS)** – A team of Scrum teams that coordinate to deliver an increment of value at the end of a sprint. In very complex scenarios, this scales to a scrum of scrum of scrums.

- **Scaled Daily Scrum (SDS)** – A method used to coordinate the SoS and ensure impediments are removed and learnings shared to achieve the sprint goal.

- **Executive Action Team (EAT)** – A team that aligns evolution of the organization to a change strategy, monitors metrics, and removes high-level impediments, and ensures decisions and priorities are addressed constantly, as decision delays are a common killer of productivity in agile settings.

- **The Agile Practice** – A cross-functional team that works across the organization to coach and train on Scrum practices to support Scrum@Scale and is a source of continuous learning for Scrum professionals.

- **The MetaScrum** – A team of POs, led by a chief product owner (CPO). It is responsible for constantly refining the product vision into a single backlog to maximize value to stakeholders through the work of the SoS. A key event is the regular MetaScrum backlog refinement meeting in which the organization aligns around a single backlog and priorities are set for multiple teams (Sutherland, 2018).

How to Determine If S@S Fits

In theory, the Scrum@Scale framework can be applied to any size or type of organization due to its scale-free architecture. In practice, there are key factors to examine to ensure that Scrum@Scale is a good fit to use as a scaling framework.

The most important factor is existing good Scrum practices. Scrum@Scale relies on the consistent and rigorous practice of Scrum as a foundation to scale. Organizations that are not truly agile will struggle with Scrum@Scale. As with Scrum itself, co-located teams are important to the success of Scrum@Scale.

Scrum@Scale is more likely to work well in organizations that have flatter organizational structures and are already accustomed to making decisions quickly. It can provide the framework for rapid prioritization and decision making but will also reveal impediments to this in more bureaucratic organizations.

Scrum@Scale is beneficial for organizations that focus on teamwork and reward collaboration. At the same time, it will reveal dysfunctional organizations focused on the individual and top-heavy structures built at the expense and loss of overall value delivery to the enterprise.

Determining If Your Organization Is Ready to Scale Agile

Attempting to scale any business practice should be carefully evaluated, and approaches to project management are no exception. Assuming that your organization has already had some success with agile, you may be thinking about whether it is time to consider scaling up your practices and processes. Perhaps you are a small firm who had been operating one scrum team, but you realize that this team has grown too large to continue as a single team. Maybe you work in a larger organization that has adopted agile in an ad hoc way, or with a degree of coordination, and now the senior leaders in the organization recognize that agile practices could serve the organization if coordinated intentionally and purposefully.

Maybe your organization has been experimenting with agile on one project using a large team and realized that one large team is not as efficient as leveraging three smaller teams on the same project but working on a single backlog. Or, perhaps you work in a government agency seeing funding cuts but with no reduction in your mission. These are just a few scenarios that I have worked in that required the organizations and their practitioners to consider one or more approaches to scaling their agile practices. There are many factors to consider.

Readiness to Change and Other Factors

With any change, the readiness and willingness of an organization to change is a critical factor. Some key factors when considering readiness to scale agile include the following:

- **Leadership support** – Leaders in an organization play a part in successful use of any scaling approach. They must be onboard with the change and accountable for supporting the work necessary.

- **Common understanding** – The organization should train its teams in agile practices with a common curriculum. A common agile language within the organization is a key when scaling agile. A common basis in training is critical.

- **Quality and rigor of existing agile practices**: The organization should already be using agile and Scrum practices with a high level of rigor and adherence to core agile and Scrum tenets.

- **Product owners (POs)** – Any organization considering scaling agile and Scrum should have embraced and implemented the concept of dedicated POs.

- **Recognition of the need** – Organizations that want to scale their agile practices should recognize the need for themselves based on empirical data and observations.

- The presence of a collaborative and servant-leadership culture in midmanagement. A culture that does not support or may even oppose key practices of agile will certainly not support any approach to scaled agile.

If some or many of these factors are missing, consider doing the work or analysis necessary to close the gaps before proceeding further with scaling agile in your organization.

Assessing Organizational Fit

LeSS is best suited for smaller to medium-sized organizations because it scales well for up to five teams at up to two sites. SAFe is better suited for large organizations, while Scrum@Scale is theoretically able to scale to any sized organization.

LeSS helps organizations delivering a single product optimize multiple Scrum teams to coordinate multiple components for a single integrated product. SAFe is designed to address the agile scaling needs of organizations with multiple products, portfolios, and programs. Scrum@Scale adapts to organizations using Scrum for developing and supporting a single product as well as to organizations delivering multiple projects with a single customer for each project.

LeSS inherently values flatter organizations and calls for a reassessment of many managerial roles as part of its implementation. SAFe acknowledges the more hierarchical models present in larger organizations while outlining ways to align the structure and agile practices to achieve scaled efficiency. Scrum@Scale scales out the Scrum model of scrum teams, scrum masters (SMs), and POs. Scrum@Scale can leverage an existing senior management structure through the creation of the EAT. Middle manager roles become less about directing work and more about supporting the teams and ensuring skills and knowledge growth for people in their functional areas.

When examining organizational models, it is also important to consider organization by product or service versus functional specialties. Organizations that are already organized along product and service lines with technology teams embedded in these lines will adapt and scale agile more easily.

Agile inherently assumes strategic input will be sought and used constantly and is designed to allow an organization to adapt to rapid change. LeSS, SAFe, and Scrum@Scale may fit better with different approaches to strategic planning. Given its likely application in smaller organizations and to a smaller number of teams, LeSS is more tolerant of shorter cycles and more frequent changes in strategic planning.

By contrast, SAFe assumes a considerable degree of architectural runway and portfolio planning. Therefore, an organization with immature strategic planning practices is not likely to realize the full benefits of SAFe. Scrum@Scale adapts to process predictability versus adaptability as well as convergence or emergence of product design. Therefore, the organization considering Scrum@Scale must consider its understanding of these aspects of its own strategy.

For example:

- Consider a company early in the adoption of agile and Scrum practices and not rigorous or disciplined in its use of agile and Scrum. No scaling should be attempted until this organization gains maturity and consistency in using agile methods.

- Consider a rapidly growing company that has used agile from the very beginning. LeSS or Scrum@Scale could work well, but this enterprise is too early in its life cycle for SAFe or may find the SAFe structures stifling.

- Consider a large national telecommunications company with 100 scrum teams delivering on many products and programs. This organization could leverage its existing scale to benefit from SAFe's structure, whereas LeSS may not be the best approach because of the multiple products and portfolios. Scrum@Scale might be theoretically possible, but likely not as good a choice as SAFe.

- Consider a recently acquired, early stage software company using agile effectively and growing its development team beyond 15 people: LeSS is a good choice because this organization is ready to split the team into two or three teams and can maintain a single PO and backlog. SAFe would not fit. Scrum@Scale would likely work, but not as well as LeSS.

Summary

Scaling your agile practices is an important decision. Recognizing when in the development and adoption of agile as a practice within your organization it is appropriate to begin scaling depends on a number of factors. Selecting the right approach is also critical. Depending on the type of company, the scale of your company, and where you are in overall maturity, one of the three approaches described here could be appropriate. Perhaps a different approach, including a hybrid approach, could be right or wrong. It may also be appropriate to look at each of these methods along with other project management and program management techniques to create a hybrid model that works for your specific situation.

Bibliography

Adkins, L. "The Scrum framework." Video file. April 1, 2011. www.youtube.com/watch?v=_BWbaZs1M_8&t=189s.

Alexander, M. "Scrum vs. lean vs. kanban: Comparing agile project management frameworks." CIO. Last modified February 28, 2017. www.cio.com/article/3175445/comparing-agile-project-management-frameworks.html?upd=1591561130118.

Ambler, Scott, and Alistair Cockburn. "Richness of Communication Channel." 2005.

Ayers, S. "Personal communications." Last modified October 13, 2016.

Berkun, S. *The Year Without Pants: WordPress.com and the Future of Work.* Hoboken, NJ: John Wiley & Sons, 2013.

Brown, T. "Design thinking." Harvard Business Review. Last modified June 1, 2008. https://hbr.org/2008/06/design-thinking.

Burnett, W. "Stanford webinar - design thinking = method, not magic." YouTube. Last modified April 20, 2016. www.youtube.com/watch?v=vSuK2C89yjA&t=30s.

Cohn, M. "Six ways a scrum master or agile coach can help the team." Last modified May 14, 2019. www.mountaingoatsoftware.com/blog/six-things-your-team-wants-from-you-as-their-scrum-master.

Cohn, M. "The ScrumMaster." Last modified 2020. www.mountaingoatsoftware.com/agile/scrum/roles/scrummaster.

© Shawn Belling 2020
S. Belling, *Succeeding with Agile Hybrids*, https://doi.org/10.1007/978-1-4842-6461-4

Cohn, M. "Cross functional doesn't mean everyone can do everything." Accessed December 28, 2019. www.mountaingoatsoftware.com/blog/cross-functional-doesnt-mean-everyone-can-do-everything.

Collyer, S., C. Warren, B. Hemsley, and C. Stevens. "Aim, fire, aim—project planning styles in dynamic environments." *Project Management Journal* 41, no. 4 (2010), 108-121. doi:10.1002/pmj.20199.

Cooper-Wright, M. "The blurring between design thinking and Agile." Medium. Last modified November 29, 2016. https://medium.com/front-line-interaction-design/the-blurring-between-design-thinking-and-agile-ae59d14f28e3.

Fewell, J. "The great debate." *PM Network* 24, no. 1 (2010), 27.

Gibbons, S. "Design thinking 101." Nielsen Norman Group. Last modified July 31, 2016. www.nngroup.com/articles/design-thinking/.

Kawasaki, Guy. "The art of innovation." *YouTube*. February 22, 2014. www.youtube.com/watch?v=Mtjatz9r-Vc.

Krause, R. "Design thinking and agile (video)." Nielsen Norman Group. n.d. www.nngroup.com/videos/design-thinking-agile/.

Larman, C., and B. Vodde. *Large-Scale Scrum: More with LeSS*. Boston, MA: Addison-Wesley Professional, 2016.

Manifesto for Agile Software Development. Accessed December 29, 2019. https://agilemanifesto.org.

Moen, R. D., and C. L. Norman. "Circling back: Clearing up the myths about the Deming cycle and seeing how it keeps evolving." Last modified 2010. www.apiweb.org/circling-back.pdf.

Norman, T. "LinkedIn feed." December 23, 2019. http://linkedin.com/feed.

Pahuja, S. "What is Scrumban?" Agile Alliance. Last modified June 22, 2017. www.agilealliance.org/what-is-scrumban/.

Rabon, B. "Five secrets to successfully implementing agile project management." n.d.

Rigby, D., J. Sutherland, and H. Takeuchi. "Embracing agile." Last modified May 1, 2016. https://hbr.org/2016/05/embracing-agile.

"Scaled Agile Framework – SAFe for lean enterprises." Accessed January 3, 2020. www.scaledagileframework.com/.

Schneider, M. "Google spent 2 years studying 180 teams. The most successful ones shared these 5 traits." Last modified July 19, 2017. www.inc.com/michael-schneider/google-thought-they-knew-how-to-create-the-perfect.html.

Schwaber, K. "SCRUM development process." Last modified 1995. `http://agilix.nl/resources/scrum_OOPSLA_95.pdf`.

Skhmot, N. "What is lean | History and early development." The Lean Way. Last modified August 5, 2017. `https://theleanway.net/what-is-lean`.

Sutherland, J. "Takeuchi and Nonaka: The roots of scrum." Last modified October 22, 2011. `www.scruminc.com/takeuchi-and-nonaka-roots-of-scrum/`.

Sutherland, J. *Scrum@Scale. Incrementally crafting the right organization*, 1st ed. Boston, MA: Scrum@Scale LLC, 2018.

Sutherland, J. "Scrum patterns by Jim Coplien: Thinking, caring, becoming." Last modified September 5, 2018. `www.scruminc.com/scrum-patterns-jim-coplien-thinking-caring-becoming/`.

Sutherland, J. "LinkedIn feed post." Last modified December 27, 2019. `http://linkedin/feed`.

Sykes, C. "LinkedIn." 2018. `www.linkedin.com/feed/update/urn:li:article:7363425453664338088?commentUrn=urn%3Ali%3Acomment%3A%28article%3A7363425453664338088%2C6472327052212129792%29`.

Takeuchi, H., and I. Nonaka. "The new new product development game." Last modified January 1986. `https://hbr.org/1986/01/the-new-new-product-development-game`.

Terry, J. "What is Kanban? | Planview LeanKit." Planview. Last modified October 3, 2018. `www.planview.com/resources/articles/what-is-kanban/`.

Thomas, Steven. "Agile Lifecycle." 2008.

Tom, S. "Living in an Agilefall world." Medium. Last modified October 8, 2019. `https://medium.com/bcg-digital-ventures/living-in-an-agilefall-world-6bc2fd94fdec`.

Index

© Shawn Belling 2020
S. Belling, *Succeeding with Agile Hybrids*, https://doi.org/10.1007/978-1-4842-6461-4